Distrust of Authority

An Anthology on Dissent

Distrust of Authority

An Anthology on Dissent

ANITA WILKES DORE • STANLEY GOTLIN

HAYDEN BOOK COMPANY, INC.
Rochelle Park, New Jersey

Library of Congress Cataloging in Publication Data

Main entry under title:

Distrust of authority.

1. Dissenters—United States—Literary collections.
2. United States—Social conditions—Sources. I. Dore, Anita Wilkes. II. Gotlin, Stanley.
PS509.D5D57 810'.8'0352 81-6832
ISBN 0-8104-6056-4 AACR2

Printed in the United States of America

1	2	3	4	5	6	7	8	9	PRINTING
81	82	83	84	85	86	87	88	89	YEAR

Preface

Does anybody out there care?

> "What difference does it make?"
> "What does it matter what I think?"
> "Who listens to me?"
> "What could I do?"

The state of our world upsets and threatens people and yet the public at large is often characterized as indifferent. Election statistics indicate a decreasing number of people cast ballots. People are fed up but feel powerless to improve the quality of their world.

Can people actually effect change? Are there examples in history and literature that demonstrate that an individual or a group can make a difference? Are there instances to prove that someone's thoughts, words, and actions actually have had an impact? Yes, there are, and we have gathered some of them in this anthology. It deals with people who took stands for what they believed in—people like W. E. B. DuBois, Lillian Hellman, Muhammed Ali, Thomas Paine, Phillip Berrigan, Martin Luther King, Phil Ochs. It will make people think about the positions they take and the commitments they fail to make. It will promote an understanding of the motives and the actions of those who are politically and socially responsive and active.

No special political or social point of view is espoused here. This anthology presents people who have rebelled against injustice, indifference, fear, status quoism. It shows people of action.

Anita Wilkes Dore
Stanley Gotlin

New York, N.Y.

Contents

INTRODUCTION

We come into this world screaming and howling at the doctor's slap. We spend our first months demanding attention and crying for food, for changing, and for comfort. As two-and-a-half-year-olds, we have an even more vigorous sense of self and say, "I want," or "I need." We are negative as well as positive at that age, and "No" is one of our favorite words. The child is strongly aware of self and is ready to stand up for what is needed or desired. As youngsters, we are quick to rebel against the authority of the parent, the babysitter, or the nursery school teacher.

That is what most of us are like at thirty months. But are we at all like that at thirty years? What happens to us as we grow older? Is the desire to express our true feelings less urgent? What pressures do we feel that make us accept without question the opinions of others and conform to beliefs the majority holds? Why do we tend to stifle our feelings of dissent? During the maturation process, we learn to control some of our demands and to censor some of our thoughts; we learn how inappropriate it is to behave like a two-year-old. How have some people been able to combine that sense of self of the child with the sense of control and responsibility of the adult?

To what extent may you be called a conformist or a rebel? Are you more likely to be labeled a bystander or an activist? Take stock of yourself by relating your experiences to the following questionnaire. Find out how much and how often you, as a citizen in a democracy, publicly express your opinions, rebel against authority, assert your rights.

	Never	*Some-times*	*Often*
1. Do you write letters to the president, a senator, or a representative protesting some proposed legislation or course of action?			
2. Do you write letters to the president, a senator, or a representative to support a controversial stand?			

	Never	*Sometimes*	*Often*
3. Do you write letters to the editor of your school newspaper or to a local newspaper to express your views on an issue?			
4. Do you ever picket a store, an embassy, or a public building?			
5. Do you respect picket lines when you see them?			
6. Have you ever gone on strike?			
7. Do you wear buttons to indicate your feeling about an explosive or controversial issue?			
8. Have you ever campaigned for a candidate?			
9. Do you wear a candidate's campaign button or display a candidate's posters or bumper stickers?			
10. Have you ever attached a bumper sticker to the family car to indicate your stand on an issue?			
11. Have you ever joined a delegation of students to visit a member of the faculty or a public official to express objections to some administrative policy?			
12. Do you attend sessions of court when a case about which you feel deeply is being tried?			
13. Have you ever carried a sign in a march to express your opinion?			
14. Have you ever participated in a vigil to express your belief that an injustice was being committed?			
15. Have you ever attended a session of the local, state, or federal legislative body or the United Nations when a heated issue was being discussed or debated?			
16. Have you ever attended a street rally when speakers were to address the public?			
17. If you are over 18, have you ever voted in a general election or in a primary?			

	Never	Sometimes	Often
18. Have you ever drawn up a petition and tried to get others to sign it?			
19. Have you ever signed someone else's petition?			
20. Have you ever asked a question of a speaker at a public meeting or at an assembly program?			
21. Have you ever challenged a teacher's grade or decision and taken your case to some other school official?			
22. Have you ever contacted a manufacturer to indicate your dissatisfaction with a product?			
23. Have you ever contacted a municipal department of consumer affairs or the Better Business Bureau of your town to complain about a faulty or misrepresented product?			

Examine your answers. Would you be classified more as an abstainer or as an activist? Are you satisfied with your record of participation? If you have done very few of these things, is it because you are entirely satisfied with the status quo? Have you ever wanted to do any of these things but didn't? Is it because you are indifferent, because you are lazy, or because you are afraid to take a stand? Are you overwhelmed by the complexity of getting involved?

All of the actions listed in the questionnaire are legal and proper methods for citizens in a democracy to express dissenting opinions. There are, however, other ways that people have made their protests known. Do you know people who have participated in any of these acts?

. . .Scribbled graffiti on sidewalks, walls, or bathrooms of public buildings.
. . .Tied up traffic defiantly.
. . .Engaged in a sit-in in a public building, office, factory, or draft board.
. . .Refused to pay taxes.
. . .Committed acts of destruction to property.
. . .Broken the law openly with acts of civil disobedience.
. . .Committed violent acts against people.
. . .Engaged in a hunger strike.

What do you think about these methods of expressing rebellion? How effective are they? What happens to people who take these courses of action? It is essential for you to examine your reactions as well as your actions. How do you feel when you witness or read about acts of dissent? Examine the acts described in the questionnaire and in the preceding paragraph. How do you react to those methods of expression? Which ones make you angry? Which ones do you support? Which ones leave you indifferent? Why?

People take stands on issues and express their feelings in many ways, both legal and illegal, sometimes effectively and sometimes ineffectively, sometimes gaining satisfaction and sometimes experiencing frustration. They do so because they're concerned enough about an issue to want to be involved. What is happening today that may concern or affect you? Are there issues at stake about which you have an opinion to express? Examine today's newspaper and mark any articles or letters to the editor that arouse an opinion from you. Is there some way to make your opinion known? Would you consider taking one of the courses of action listed in the questionnaire you just answered?

We are living in a country witp a long history of rebellion and dissent. Flip through the pages of any history book and you will find many rebels in American history, some of whom have been canonized for their actions and for their words. This book contains many expressions of dissent and rebellion on a broad range of subjects, by and about real and fictional rebels. What they have said and done has shaped the destiny of this country. What they have said and done has also influenced the way you think, speak, and act. Although some of these people lived years ago, there is no topic included that does not affect us all today. The recording of their deeds and the recollection of their words will motivate you to question your future actions and attitudes.

1

CONFORMITY

What do nonconformists look like? How do they dress? Take a moment to form a picture of them. Did you visualize people with long, unkempt hair pulled back in a ponytail tied with a rubberband or swept back half off the forehead and held by a colored headband? Did you picture women who were bra-less under their tie-dyed tee shirts or their loose, bleached gauze blouses? Did you see men whose faces were dominated by untrimmed beards and mustaches?

If we see nonconformists as dressing in a standard way or in a "uniform," what are we saying about their nonconformity? Why do they wear a "uniform"? Are they like the rest of us who wear some type of uniform and who follow the crowd in other ways? What is the "uniform" in your school or neighborhood?

When you pictured nonconformists before, did you see women in matched skirts, blouses, and jackets; women whose hair was perfectly combed? Did you see men in dark three-piece suits, men whose hair was neither particularly long nor excessively short? Did you picture people you might see portraying parents in such television series as "Family," "Happy Days," or "Father Knows Best"?

Many people find it difficult to believe that a person who expresses a nonconforming idea can look like an average person. For some reason, they derive satisfaction in thinking that a person who speaks out on an issue is strange and therefore looks strange. Jane Fonda, William Kuntsler, and Jerry Brown are three people who have been speaking out and taking stands on controversial issues. They look like most people and dress in an ordinary, though fashionable, way. How would people react to them or their ideas if they dressed or behaved unconventionally?

Conformity exists not only externally, as shown in patterns of dress, but also internally, as shown in patterns of thought and behavior. What do people think will happen to them if they do not conform? The answer to that question should explain the appeal of the uniform, the appeal of conformity.

from "The Mysterious Stranger" *by Mark Twain*

Mark Twain is perhaps best known for his novels Tom Sawyer *and* Huckleberry Finn *and other works set in America. However, "The Mysterious Stranger," his last major work, is set in a mythical mid-European country. It exemplifies the use of satire and wit for which he is known.*

Have you read about the frenzy surrounding the Salem witch trials? About the zeal with which some joined Senator Joseph McCarthy in his search for communists in America in the 1950s? Mark Twain has Satan observe the actions of people during a particular event. His comments will help you to understand why such events take place.

* * *

It was wonderful, the mastery Satan had over time and distance. For him they did not exist. He called them human inventions, and said they were artificialities. We often went to the most distant parts of the globe with him, and stayed weeks and months, and yet were gone only a fraction of a second, as a rule. You could prove it by the clock. One day when our people were in such awful distress because the witch commission were afraid to proceed against the astrologer and Father Peter's household, or against any indeed, but the poor and the friendless, they lost patience and took to witch hunting on their own score, and began to chase a born lady who was known to have the habit of curing people by devilish arts, such as bathing them, washing them, and nourishing them instead of bleeding them and purging them through the ministrations of a barber-surgeon in the proper way. She came flying down, with the howling and cursing mob after her, and tried to take refuge in houses, but the doors were shut in her face. They chased her more than half an hour, we following to see it, and at last she was exhausted and fell, and they caught her. They dragged her to a tree and threw a rope over the limb, and began to make a noose in it, some holding her, meantime, and she crying and begging, and her young daughter looking on and weeping, but afraid to say or do anything.

They hanged the lady, and I threw a stone at her, although in my heart I was sorry for her; but all were throwing stones and each was watching his neighbor, and if I had not done as the others did it would have been noticed and spoken of. Satan burst out laughing.

All that were near by turned upon him, astonished and not pleased. It was an ill time to laugh, for his free and scoffing ways and his supernatural music had brought him under suspicion all over the town and turned many privately against him. The big blacksmith called attention to him now, raising his voice so that all should hear, and said:

"What are you laughing at? Answer! Moreover, please explain to the company why you threw no stone."

"Are you sure I did not throw a stone?"

"Yes. You needn't try to get out of it; I had my eye on you."

"And I—I noticed you!" shouted two others.

"Three witnesses," said Satan: "Mueller, the blacksmith; Klein, the butcher's man; Pfeiffer, the weaver's journeyman. Three very ordinary liars. Are there any more?"

"Never mind whether there are others or not, and never mind about what you consider us—three's enough to settle your matter for you. You'll prove that you threw a stone, or it shall go hard with you."

"That's so!" shouted the crowd, and surged up as closely as they could to the center of interest.

"And first you will answer that other question," cried the blacksmith, pleased with himself for being mouthpiece to the public and hero of the occasion. "What are you laughing at?"

Satan smiled and answered, pleasantly: "To see three cowards stoning a dying lady when they were so near death themselves."

You could see the superstitious crowd shrink and catch their breath, under the sudden shock. The blacksmith, with a show of bravado, said:

"Pooh! What do you know about it?"

"I? Everything. By profession I am a fortune-teller, and I read the hands of you three—and some others—when you lifted them to stone the woman. One of you will die to-morrow week; another of you will die to-night; the third has but five minutes to live—and yonder is the clock!"

It made a sensation. The faces of the crowd blanched, and turned mechanically toward the clock. The butcher and the weaver seemed smitten with an illness, but the blacksmith braced up and said, with spirit:

"It is not long to wait for prediction number one. If it fails, young master, you will not live a whole minute after, I promise you that."

No one said anything; all watched the clock in a deep stillness which was impressive. When four and a half minutes were gone the blacksmith gave a sudden gasp and clapped his hands upon his heart, saying, "Give me breath! Give me room!" and began to sink down. The crowd surged back, no one offering to support him, and he fell lumbering to the ground and was dead. The people stared at him, then at Satan, then at one another; and their lips moved, but no words came. Then Satan said:

"Three saw that I threw no stone. Perhaps there are others; let them speak."

It struck a kind of panic into them, and, although no one answered him, many began to violently accuse one another, saying, "You said he didn't throw," and getting for reply, "It is a lie, and I will make you eat it!" And so in a moment they were in a raging and noisy turmoil, and beating and banging one another; and in the midst was the only indifferent one—the dead lady hanging from her rope, her troubles forgotten, her spirit at peace.

So we walked away, and I was not at ease, but was saying to myself, "He told them he was laughing at them, but it was lie—he was laughing at me."

That made him laugh again, and he said, "Yes, I was laughing at you, because, in fear of what others might report about you, you stoned the woman when your heart revolted at the act—but I was laughing at the others, too."

"Why?"

"Because their case was yours."

"How is that?"

"Well, there were sixty-eight people there, and sixty-two of them had no more desire to throw a stone than you had."

"Satan!"

"Oh, it's true. I know your race. It is made up of sheep. It is governed by minorities, seldom or never by majorities. It suppresses its feelings and its beliefs and follows the handful that makes the most noise. Sometimes the noisy handful is right, sometimes wrong, but no matter, the crowd follows it. The vast majority of the race, whether savage or civilized, are secretly kind-hearted and shrink from inflicting pain, but in the presence of the aggressive and pitiless minority they don't dare to assert themselves. Think of it! One kind-hearted creature spies upon another, and sees to it that he loyally helps in iniquities which revolt both of them. Speaking as an expert, I know that ninety-nine out of a hundred of your race were strongly against the killing of witches when that foolishness was first agitated by a handful of pious lunatics in the long ago. And I know that even to-day, after ages of transmitted prejudice and silly teaching, only one person in twenty puts any real heart into the harrying of a witch. And yet apparently everybody hates witches and wants them killed. Some day a handful will rise up on the other side and make the most noise—perhaps even a single daring man with a big voice and a determined front will do it—and in a week all the sheep will wheel and follow him, and witch-hunting will come to a sudden end.

"Monarchies, aristocracies, and religions are all based upon that large defect in your race—the individual's distrust of his neighbor, and his desire, for safety's or comfort's sake, to stand well in his neighbor's eye. These institutions will always remain, and always flourish, and always oppress you, affright you, and degrade you, because you will always be and remain slaves of minorities. There was never a country where the majority of the people were in their secret hearts loyal to any of these institutions."

I did not like to hear our race called sheep, and said I did not think they were.

"Still, it is true, lamb," said Satan. "Look at you in war—what mutton you are, and how ridiculous!"

"In war? How?"

"There has never been a just one, never an honorable one—on the part of the instigator of the war. I can see a million years ahead, and this rule will never change in so many as half a dozen instances. The loud little handful—as usual—will shout for the war. The pulpit will—warily and cautiously—object—at first; the great, big, dull bulk of the nation will rub its sleepy eyes and try to make out why there should be a war, and will say, earnestly and indignantly, 'It is unjust and dishonorable, and there is no necessity for it.' Then the handful will shout louder. A few fair men on the other side will argue and reason against the war with speech and pen, and at first will have a hearing and be applauded; but it will not last long; those others will outshout them, and presently the anti-war audiences will thin out and lose popularity. Before long you will see this curious thing: the speakers stoned from the platform, and free speech strangled by hordes of furious men who in their secret hearts are still at one with those stoned speakers—as earlier—but do not dare to say so. And now the whole nation—pulpit and all—will take up the war-cry, and shout itself hoarse, and mob any honest man who ventures to open his mouth; and presently such mouths will cease to open. Next the statesmen will invent cheap lies, putting the blame upon the nation that is attacked, and every man will be glad those conscience-soothing falsities, and will diligently study them, and refuse to examine any refutations of them; and thus he will by and by convince himself that the war is just, and will thank God for the better sleep he enjoys after this process of grotesque self-deception."

"Much Madness Is Divinest Sense" *by Emily Dickinson*

Use the resources of your school or local library to discover the details of Emily Dickinson's life. When you learn about her life in detail, you may think her eccentric. If you do, you will find that she is speaking to you in this poem.

* * *

Much madness is divinest sense
To a discerning eye;
Much sense the starkest madness.

'Tis the majority
In this, as all, prevails.
Assent, and you are sane;
Demur,—you're straightway dangerous,
And handled with a chain.

from **One Flew Over the Cuckoo's Nest** *by Ken Kesey*

McMurphy, "Mack," has been ordered to undergo psychiatric observation. Is he truly "mad" or is he acting so to avoid jail? While he is undergoing the observation process, we see how Mack interacts with other patients and attempts to influence their actions. In this novel, the sanity of the authorities who judge the sanity of others is often questioned.

* * *

There's long spells—three days, years— when you can't see a thing, know where you are only by the speaker sounding overhead like a bell buoy clanging in the fog. When I can see, the guys are usually moving around as unconcerned as though they didn't notice so much as a mist in the air. I believe the fog affects their memory some way it doesn't affect mine.

Even McMurphy doesn't seem to know he's been fogged in. If he does, he makes sure not to let on that he's bothered by it. He's making sure none of the staff sees him bothered by anything; he knows that there's no better way in the world to aggravate somebody who's trying to make it hard for you than by acting like you're not bothered.

He keeps up his high-class manners around the nurses and the black boys in spite of anything they might say to him, in spite of every trick they pull to get him to lose his temper. A couple of times some stupid rule gets him mad, but he just makes himself act more polite and mannerly than ever till he begins to see how funny the whole thing is—the rules, the disapproving looks they use to enforce the rules, the ways of talking to you like you're nothing but a three-year-old—and when he sees how funny it is he goes to laughing, and this aggravates them no end. He's safe as long as he can laugh, he thinks, and it works pretty fair. Just once he loses control and shows he's mad, and then it's not because of the black boys or the Big Nurse and something they did, but it's because of the patients, and something they *didn't* do.

It happened at one of the group meetings. He got mad at the guys for acting too cagey—too chicken-shit, he called it. He'd been taking bets from all of them on the World Series coming up Friday. He'd had it in mind that they would get to watch the games on TV, even though they didn't come on during regulation TV time. During the meeting a few days before he asks if it wouldn't be okay if they did the cleaning work at night, during TV time, and watched the games during the afternoon. The nurse tells him no, which is about what he expected. She tells him how the schedule has been set up for a delicately balanced reason that would be thrown into turmoil by the switch of routines.

This doesn't surprise him, coming from the nurse; what does surprise him is how the Acutes act when he asks them what they think of the idea. Nobody says a thing. They're all sunk back out of sight in little pockets of fog. I can barely see them.

"Now look here," he tells them, but they don't look. He's been waiting for somebody to say something, answer his question. Nobody acts like they've heard it. "Look here, damn it," he says when nobody moves, "there's at least twelve of you guys I know of myself got a leetle personal *interest* who wins these games. Don't you guys care to watch them?"

"I don't know, Mack," Scanlon finally says, "I'm pretty used to seeing that six-o'clock news. And if switching times would really mess up the schedule as bad as Miss Ratched says—"

"The hell with the schedule. You can get back to the bloody schedule next week, when the Series is over. What do you say, buddies? Let's take a vote on watching the TV during the afternoon instead of at night. All those in favor?"

"Ay," Cheswick calls out and gets to his feet.

"I mean all those in favor raise their hands. Okay, all those in favor?"

Cheswick's hand comes up. Some of the other guys look around to see if there's any other fools. McMurphy can't believe it.

"Come on now, what is this crap? I thought you guys could vote on policy and that sort of thing. Isn't that the way it is, Doc?"

The doctor nods without looking up.

"Okay then; now who wants to watch those games?"

Cheswick shoves his hand higher and glares around. Scanlon shakes his head and then raises his hand, keeping his elbow on the arm of the chair. And nobody else. McMurphy can't say a word.

"If that's settled, then," the nurse says, "perhaps we should get on with the meeting."

"Yeah," he says, slides down in his chair till the brim of his cap nearly touches his chest. "Yeah, perhaps we should get on with the sonofabitchin' meeting at that."

"Yeah," Cheswick says, giving all the guys a hard look and sitting down, "yeah, get on with the godblessed meeting." He nods stiffly, then settles his chin down on his chest, scowling. He's pleased to be sitting next to McMurphy, feeling brave like this. It's the first time Cheswick ever had somebody along with him on his lost causes.

After the meeting McMurphy won't say a word to any of them, he's so mad and disgusted. It's Billy Bibbit who goes up to him.

"Some of us have b-been here for fi-fi-five years, Randle," Billy says. He's got a magazine rolled up and is twisting at it with his hands; you can see the cigarette burns on the backs of his hands. "And some of us will b-be here maybe th-that muh-muh-much longer, long after you're g-g-gone, long after this Wo-world Series is over. And . . . don't you see . . ." He throws down the magazine and walks away. "Oh, what's the use of it anyway."

McMurphy stares after him, that puzzled frown knotting his bleached eyebrows together again.

He argues for the rest of the day with some of the other guys about why they didn't vote, but they don't want to talk about it, so he seems to give up, doesn't say anything about it again till the day before the Series starts. "Here it is Thursday," he says, sadly shaking his head.

He's sitting on one of the tables in the tub room with his feet on a chair, trying to spin his cap around one finger. Other Acutes mope around the room and try not to pay any attention to him. Nobody'll play poker or blackjack with him for money any more—after the patients wouldn't vote he got mad and skinned them so bad at cards that they're all so in debt they're scared to go any deeper—and they can't play for cigarettes because the nurse has started making the men keep their cartons on the desk in the Nurses' Station, where she doles them out one pack a day, says it's for their health, but everybody knows it's to keep McMurphy from winning them all at cards. With no poker or blackjack, it's quiet in the tub room, just the sound of the speaker drifting in from the day room. It's so quiet you can hear that guy upstairs in Disturbed climbing the wall, giving out an occasional signal, loo loo *looo,* a bored, uninterested sound, like a baby yells to yell itself to sleep.

"Thursday," McMurphy says again.

"*Looooo,*" yells that guy upstairs.

"That's Rawler," Scanlon says, looking up at the ceiling. He don't want to pay any attention to McMurphy. "Rawler the Squawler. He came through this ward a few years back. Wouldn't keep still to suit Miss Ratched, you remember, Billy? Loo loo loo all the time till I thought I'd go nuts. What they should do with that whole bunch of dingbats up there is toss a couple of grenades in the dorm. They're no use to anybody—"

"And tomorrow is Friday," McMurphy says. He won't let Scanlon change the subject.

"Yeah," Cheswick says, scowling around the room, "tomorrow is Friday,"

Harding turns a page of his magazine, "And that will make nearly a week our friend McMurphy has been with us without succeeding in throwing over the government, is that what you're saying Cheswickle? Lord, to think of the chasm of apathy in which we have fallen—a shame, a pitiful shame."

"The hell with that," McMurphy says. "What Cheswick means is that the first Series game is gonna be played on TV tomorrow, and what are we gonna be doin'? Mopping up this damned nursery again."

"Yeah," Cheswick says, "Ol' Mother Ratched's Therapeutic Nursery."

Against the wall of the tub room I get a feeling like a spy; the mop handle in my hands is made of metal instead of wood (metal's a better conductor) and it's hollow; there's plenty of room inside it to hide a miniature microphone. If the Big Nurse is hearing this, she'll really get Cheswick. I take a hard ball of gum from my pocket and pick some fuzz off it and hold it in my mouth till it softens.

"Let me see again," McMurphy says. "How many of you birds will vote with me if I bring up that time switch again?"

About half the Acutes nod yes, a lot more than would really vote. He puts his hat back on his head and leans his chin in his hands.

"I tell ya, I can't figure it out. Harding, what's wrong with *you,* for crying out loud? You afraid if you raise your hand that old buzzard'll cut it off."

Harding lifts one thin eyebrow. "Perhaps I am; perhaps I *am* afraid she'll cut it off if I raise it."

"What about you, Billy? Is that what you're scared of?"

"No. I don't think she'd d-d-*do* anything, but"—he shrugs and sighs and climbs up on the big panel that controls the nozzles on the shower, perches up there like a monkey—"but I just don't think a vote wu-wu-would do any good. Not in the l-long run. It's just no use, M-Mack."

"Do any *good*? Hooee! It'd do you birds some good just to get the exercise lifting that arm."

"It's still a risk, my friend. She always has the capacity to make things worse for us. A baseball game isn't worth the risk," Harding says.

"Who the hell says so? Jesus, I haven't missed a World Series in years. Even when I was in the cooler one September they let us bring in a TV and watch the *Series;* they'd of had a riot on their hands if they hadn't. I just may have to kick that damned door down and walk to some bar downtown to see the game, just me and my buddy Cheswick."

"Now there's a suggestion with a lot of merit," Harding says, tossing down his magazine. "Why not bring that up for vote in group meeting tomorrow? 'Miss Ratched, I'd like to move that the ward be transported *en masse* to the Idle Hour for beer and television.' "

"I'd second the motion," Cheswick says. "Damn right."

"The hell with that in mass business," McMurphy says. "I'm tired of looking at you bunch of old ladies; when me and Cheswick bust outta here I think by God I'm gonna nail the door shut behind me. You guys better stay behind; your mamma probably wouldn't let you cross the street."

"Yeah? Is that it?" Fredrickson has come up behind McMurphy. "You're just going to raise one of those big he-man boots of yours and *kick* down the door? A real tough guy."

McMurphy don't hardly look at Fredrickson; he's learned that Fredrickson might act hard-boiled now and then but it's an act that folds under the slightest scare.

"What about it, he-man," Fredrickson keeps on, "are you going to kick down that door and show us how tough you are?"

"No, Fred, I guess not. I wouldn't want to scuff up my boot."

"Yeah? Okay, you been talking so big, just how *would* you go about busting out of here?"

McMurphy takes a look around him. "Well, I guess I could knock the mesh outa one of these windows with a chair when and if I took a notion. . . ."

"Yeah? You could, could you? Knock it right out? Okay, let's see you try. Come on, he-man, I'll bet you ten dollars you can't do it."

"Don't bother trying, Mack," Cheswick says. "Fredickson knows you'll just break a chair and end up on Disturbed. The first day we arrived over here we were given a demonstration about these screens. They're specially made. A technician picked up a chair just like that one you've got your feet on and beat the screen till the chair was no more than kindling wood. Didn't hardly dent the screen."

"Okay then," McMurphy says, taking a look around him. I can see he's getting more interested. I hope the Big Nurse isn't hearing this; he'll be up on Disturbed in an hour. "We need something heavier. How about a table?"

"Same as the chair. Same wood, same weight."

"All right, by God, let's just figure out what I'd have to toss through that screen to bust out. And if you birds don't think I'd do it if I ever got the urge, then you got another think coming. Okay—something bigger'n a table or a chair . . . Well, if it was night I might throw that fat coon through it; he's heavy enough."

"Much too soft," Harding says. "He'd hit the screen and it would dice him like an eggplant."

"How about one of the beds?"

"A bed is too big even if you could lift it. It wouldn't go through the window."

"I could lift it all right. Well, hell, right over there you are: that thing Billy's sittin' on. That big control panel with all the handles and cranks. That's hard enough, ain't it? And it damn well should be heavy enough."

"Sure," Fredrickson says. "That's the same as you kicking your foot through the steel door at the front."

"What would be wrong with using the panel? It don't look nailed down."

"No, it's not bolted—there's probably nothing holding it but a few wires—but *look* at it, for Christsakes."

Everybody looks. The panel is steel and cement, half the size of one of the tables, probably weighs four hundred pounds.

"Okay, I'm looking at it. It don't look any bigger than hay bales I've bucked up onto truck beds."

"I'm afraid, my friend, that this contrivance will weigh a bit more than your bales of hay."

"About a quarter-ton more, I'd bet," Fredrickson says.

"He's right, Mack," Cheswick says. "It'd be awful heavy."

"Hell, are you birds telling me I can't *lift* that dinky little gizmo?"

"My friend, I don't recall anything about psychopaths being able to move mountains in addition to their other noteworthy assets."

"Okay, you say I can't lift it. Well *by* God . . ."

McMurphy hops off the table and goes to peeling off his green jacket; the tattoos sticking half out of his T-shirt jump around the muscles on his arms.

"Then who's willing to lay five bucks? Nobody's gonna convince me I can't do something till I try it. Five bucks . . ."

"McMurphy, this is as foolhardy as your bet about the nurse."

"Who's got five bucks they want to lose? You hit or you sit. . . ."

The guys all go to signing liens at once; he's beat them so many times at poker and blackjack they can't wait to get back at him, and this is a certain sure thing. I don't know what he's driving at; broad and big as he is, it'd take three of him to move that panel, and he knows it. He can just look at it and see he probably couldn't even tip it, let alone lift it. It'd take a giant to lift it off the ground. But when the Acutes all get their IOUs signed, he steps up to the panel and lifts Billy Bibbit down off it and spits in his big callused palms and slaps them together, rolls his shoulders.

"Okay, stand outa the way. Sometimes when I go to exertin' myself I use up all the air nearby and grown men faint from suffocation. Stand back. There's liable to be crackin' cement and flying steel. Get the women and kids someplace safe. Stand back. . . ."

"By golly, he might do it," Cheswick mutters.

"Sure, maybe he'll talk it off the floor," Fredrickson says.

"More likely he'll acquire a beautiful hernia," Harding says. "Come now, McMurphy, quit acting like a fool; there's no man can lift that thing."

"Stand back, sissies, you're using my oxygen."

McMurphy shifts his feet a few times to get a good stance, and wipes his hands on his thighs again, then leans down and gets hold of the levers on each side of the panel. When he goes to straining, the guys go to hooting and kidding him. He turns loose and straightens up and shifts his feet around again.

"Giving up?" Fredrickson grins.

"Just *limbering* up. Here goes the real effort"—and grabs those levers again.

And suddenly nobody's hooting at him any more. His arms commence to swell, and the veins squeeze up to the surface. He clinches his eyes, and his lips draw away from his teeth. His head leans back, and tendons stand out like coiled ropes running from his heaving neck down both arms to his hands. His whole body shakes with the strain as he tries to lift something he *knows* he can't lift, something *everybody* knows he can't lift.

But, for just a second, when we hear the cement grind at our feet, we think, by golly, he might do it.

Then his breath explodes out of him, and he falls back limp against the wall. There's blood on the levers where he tore his hands. He pants for a minute against the wall with his eyes shut. There's no sound but his scraping breath; nobody's saying a thing.

He opens his eyes and looks around at us. One by one he looks at the guys—even at me—then he fishes in his pockets for all the IOUs he won the last few days at poker. He bends over the table and tries to sort them, but his hands are froze into red claws, and he can't work the fingers.

Finally he throws the whole bundle on the floor—probably forty or fifty dollars' worth from each man—and turns to walk out of the tub room. He stops at the door and looks back at everybody standing around.

"But I tried, though," he says. "Goddammit, I sure as hell did that much, now, didn't I?"

And walks out and leaves those stained pieces of paper on the floor for whoever wants to sort through them.

Topics for Discussion, Research, and Composition

1. How is Mark Twain using satire when he describes the "devilish arts" used by the lady to cure people? Investigate medical practices of earlier centuries. What was the "scientific" principle behind each practice? How did they actually hasten the patient's death or prolong illness?
2. Stoning a person to death is a form of punishment referred to in other works. Read "The Lottery" by Shirley Jackson to find a chilling account of such a practice. "He that is without sin among you, let him first cast a stone. . . ." (John 8:7) How is this line meant to influence a crowd about to stone a person?

3. a. Satan says that our race is "made up of sheep . . . governed by minorities." Describe how this is true in the fashion industry, in the various fields of entertainment, in the art world, and in politics.
   b. Many advertisements employ the "bandwagon" technique. How is it used to influence the shopping habits of the consumer? Create some slogans aimed at "a nation of sheep."
4. Investigate the influence of public opinion on the involvement of the United States in Vietnam. In what way is Mark Twain's comment about war applicable to the movement that generated a war effort and, later on, generated a peace effort?
5. Find the sections of Mark Twain's selection that parallel the feelings expressed by Emily Dickinson. In what ways are they similar?
6. One of the characters in *One Flew Over the Cuckoo's Nest* reveals another reason for conforming. How do Harding and the other men explain their conformity?
7. McMurphy attempts what is seen as an impossible task. If the others saw the futility of his act, he must have recognized it also. What satisfaction did he derive from his attempt? What is he attempting to demonstrate to the others?
8. Describe some examples of conformity that you have witnessed in school or in other places and situations.

2

LAW AND GOVERNMENT

The people of the United States, like the people in other countries, live under the control of the government and abide by a series of laws. The government and the people form a symbiotic relationship: The government derives its legitimacy and its revenues from the people; the people are, in turn, protected and served by the government and the laws it writes.

What happens when the government no longer serves the needs of its people? What happens when the government no longer serves the needs of some of its people? What happens when the government no longer serves your needs?

If a government allows its citizens to disobey its laws with impunity, can the government effectively endure? If an individual cannot abide by a governmental decision or support a given law in good conscience, must that person obey that decision or law, or is the individual responsible to an even higher authority?

The way a government responds to such challenges to its author ty often identifies the character of that government and its leaders. The way an individual responds to such challenges to conscience often identifies the character and the integrity of that individual.

from **"Common Sense"** *by Thomas Paine*

It made perfectly good sense, to Thomas Paine, that America be completely independent from England and that a strong federal union be established. His ideas, expressed in Common Sense, *outlined the colonists' cause and influenced the political thinking of many of the leaders of the Revolution.*

Why do all countries have formal governments? What do such governments do for the people? Why has it been impossible for people to survive without a formal ruling body? What is gained and lost by having a formal government?

* * *

Some writers have so confounded society with government, as to leave little or no distinction between them; whereas they are not only different, but have different origins. Society is produced by our wants and government by our wickedness; the former promotes our happiness *positively* by uniting our affections, the latter *negatively* by restraining our vices. The one encourages intercourse, the other creates distinctions. The first is a patron, the last a punisher.

Society in every state is a blessing but government, even in its best state, is but a necessary evil; in its worst state an intolerable one: for when we suffer, or are exposed to the same miseries by a *government*, which we might expect in a country *without government*, our calamity is heightened by reflecting that we furnish the means by which we suffer. Government, like dress, is the badge of lost innocence; the palaces of kings are built upon the ruins of the bowers of paradise. For were the impulses of conscience clear, uniform and irresistibly obeyed, man would need no other lawgiver; but that not being the case, he finds it necessary to surrender up a part of his property to furnish means for the protection of the rest; and this he is induced to do by the same prudence which in every other case advises him, out of two evils to choose the least. Wherefore, security being the true design and end of government, it unanswerably follows that whatever form thereof appears most likely to ensure it to us, with the least expense and greatest benefit, is preferable to all others.

In order to gain a clear and just idea of the design and end of government, let us suppose a small number of persons settled in some sequestered part of the earth, unconnected with the rest; they will then represent the first peopling of any country, or of the world. In this state of natural liberty, society will be their first thought. A thousand motives will excite them thereto; the strength of one man is so unequal to his wants, and his mind so unfitted for perpetual solitude, that he is soon obliged to seek assistance and relief of another, who in his turn requires the same. Four or five united would be able to raise a tolerable dwelling in the midst of a wilderness, but one man might labour out the common period of life without accomplishing anything; when he had felled his timber he could not remove it, nor erect it after it was removed; hunger in the mean time would urge him to quit his work, and every different want would call him a different way. Disease, nay even misfortune, would be death; for though neither might be mortal, yet either would disable him from living, and reduce him to a state in which he might rather be said to perish than to die.

Thus necessity, like a gravitating power, would soon form our newly arrived emigrants into society, the reciprocal blessings of which would supersede, and render the obligations of law and government unnecessary while they remained perfectly just to each other; but as nothing but Heaven is impregnable to vice, it will unavoidably happen that in proportion as they surmount the first difficulties of emigration, which bound them together in a common cause, they will begin to relax in their duty and attachment to each other: and this remissness will point out the necessity of establishing some form of government to supply the defect of moral virtue.

from **"Civil Disobedience"** *by Henry David Thoreau*

Thoreau once went to jail because he refused to pay taxes at a time when he knew those taxes were financing the United States' war with Mexico; he believed that that war was wrong and immoral. The reasons for his actions are clear in this selection.

* * *

I heartily accept the motto,—"That government is best which governs least;" and I should like to see it acted up to more rapidly and systematically. Carried out, it finally amounts to this, which also I believe,—"That government is best which governs not at all;" and when men are prepared for it, that will be the kind of government which they will have. Government is at best but an expedient; but most governments are usually, and all governments are sometimes, inexpedient. The objections which have been brought against a standing army, and they are many and weighty, and deserve to prevail, may also at last be brought against a standing government. The standing army is only an arm of the standing government. The government itself, which is only the mode which the people have chosen to execute their will, is equally liable to be abused and perverted before the people can act through it. Witness the present Mexican war, the work of comparatively a few individuals using the standing government as their tool; for, in the outset, the people would not have consented to this measure.

This American government,—what is it but a tradition, though a recent one, endeavoring to transmit itself unimpaired to posterity, but each instant losing some of its integrity? It has not the vitality and force of a single living man; for a single man can bend it to his will. It is a sort of wooden gun to the people themselves. But it is not the less necessary for this; for the people must have some complicated machinery or other, and hear its din, to satisfy that idea of government which they have. Governments show thus how successfully men can be imposed on, even impose on themselves, for their own advantage. It is excellent, we must all allow. Yet this government never of itself furthered any enterprise, but by the alacrity with which it got out of its way. *It* does not keep the country free. *It* does not settle the West. *It* does not educate. The character inherent in the American people has done all that has been accomplished; and it would have done somewhat more, if the government had not sometimes got its way. For government is an expedient by which men would fain succeed in letting one another alone; and, as has been said, when it is most expedient, the governed are most let alone by it. Trade and commerce, if they were not made of India-rubber, would never manage to bounce over the obstacles which legislators are continually putting in their way; and, if one were to judge these men wholly by the effects of their actions and not partly by their intentions, they would deserve to be classed and punished with those mischievous persons who put obstructions on the railroads.

But, to speak practially and as a citizen, unlike those who call themselves no-government men, I ask for, not at once no government, but *at once* a better government. Let every man make known what kind of government would command his respect, and that will be one step toward obtaining it.

After all, the practical reason why, when the power is once in the hands of the people, a majority are permitted, and for a long period continue, to rule is not because they are most likely to be in the right, nor because this seems fairest to the minority, but because they are physically the strongest. But a government in which the majority rule in all cases cannot be based on justice, even as far as men understand it. Can there not be a government in which majorities do not virtually decide right and wrong, but conscience?—in which majorities decide only those questions to which the rule of expediency is applicable? Must the citizen ever for a moment, or in the least degree, resign his conscience to the legislator? Why has every man a conscience, then? I think that we should be men first, and subjects afterward. It is not desirable to cultivate a respect for the law, so much as for the right. The only obligation which I have a right to assume is to do at any time what I think right. It is truly enough said, that a corporation has no conscience; but a corporation of conscientious men is a corporation *with* a conscience. Law never made men a whit more just; and, by means of their respect for it, even the well-disposed are daily made the agents of injustice. A common and natural result of an undue respect for law is, that you may see a file of soldiers, colonel, captain, corporal, privates, powder-monkeys, and all, marching in admirable order over hill and dale to the wars, against their wills, ay, against their common sense and consciences, which makes it very steep marching indeed, and produces a palpitation of the heart. They have no doubt that it is a damnable business in which they are concerned; they are all peaceably inclined. Now, what are they? Men at all? Or small movable forts and magazines, at the service of some unscrupulous man in power? . . .

How does it become a man to behave toward this American government to-day? I answer, that he cannot without disgrace be associated with it. I cannot for an instant recognize that political organization as *my* government which is the *slave's* government also.

All men recognize the right of revolution; that is, the right to refuse allegiance to, and to resist, the government, when its tyranny or its inefficency are great and unendurable. But almost all say that such is not the case now. But such was the case, they think, in the Revolution of '75. If one were to tell me that this was a bad government because it taxed certain foreign commodities brought to its ports, it is most probable that I should not make an ado about it, for I can do without them. All machines have their friction; and possibly this does enough good to counterbalance the evil. At any rate, it is a great evil to make a stir about it. But when the friction comes to have its machine, and oppression and robbery are organized, I say, let us not have such a machine any longer. In other words, when a sixth of the population of a nation which has undertaken to be the refuge of liberty are slaves, and a whole country is unjustly overrun and conquered by a foreign army, and subjected to military law, I think that it is not too soon for honest men to rebel and revolutionize. What makes this duty the more urgent is the fact that the country so overrun is not our own, but ours is the invading army.

"Reply to Abe Fortas" *by Howard Zinn*

Abe Fortas was a Justice of the United States Supreme Court in the 1960s. During that decade there were many acts of civil disobedience committed in the country. He wrote that the law was to be obeyed even if one disagreed with it. This selection is the response of a historian to that opinion.

In July 1977, New York City endured a twenty-four-hour electrical power blackout. During that time, stores in the city's poverty areas were looted and destroyed. Was this civil disobedience or riot? Zinn draws distinctions between these terms and also shows their interrelatedness.

* * *

But there can be no moral imperative to obey an immoral law, unless the very idea of obedience to law, in general, has an overriding moral value. Any intelligent assessment of the right of civil disobedience must probe exactly that point: How much weight—if any at all—should be given the general principle of obedience to law, so that we will know when it outweighs the moral necessity to disobey an unjust law.

Let us be clear: It is not hard to show that there is value to specific good laws; they fix, strengthen, remind us of some moral proposition, like that against murder, against driving recklessly on a public highway, against barring someone from a public place because of his race. But does the idea of obedience to law *in general* have such a high intrinsic value that the law must be held sacrosanct even where it violates an important human right or protects an evil condition?

Most of us do have some commitment to the rule of law in general. Our reasons go deep into the past. From the Magna Carta on, the idea grew that a code of laws could serve to limit the arbitrary rule of kings and tyrants, define the limits of the ruler's power, and declare the rights of the citizen.

Indeed, laws may do this. But laws, even where parliamentary government has replaced monarchy, may also enhance the power of the ruler and violate the rights of the citizen. To assume that because some laws may serve democratic purposes all laws must always be obeyed, is to give a blank check to government—something that citizens in a democracy should never do.

A common argument is that disobedience even of bad laws is wrong because that fosters a general disrespect for all laws, including good ones, which we need. But this is like arguing that children should be made to eat rotten fruit along with the good, lest they get the idea *all* fruit should be thrown away. Isn't it likely that someone forced to eat the rotten fruit may because of that develop a distaste for all fruit?

In fact, there is no evidence that violations of law in the spirit of civil disobedience lead to a general contempt for all laws. If this were so, we might expect either that persons engaging in civil disobedience become general law violators, or that other persons are encouraged by these acts to become indiscriminate violators of law. There is no indication that this has happened. For instance, Negroes in the South who began to violate segregation laws in organized campaigns of civil disobedience did not at the same time become general lawbreakers, nor did this lead to a larger crime rate among others in the population. Indeed, it was found in Albany, Georgia, that during the mass demonstrations of civil disobedience there in 1961 and 1962, the general crime rate declined.

The danger is in the other direction. When laws which violate the human spirit are maintained (like the segregation laws), or intolerable conditions are protected by the rule of law (like the poverty of Harlem amidst the wealth of Manhattan), and the victims have not found an *organized* way of protesting via civil disobedience, some will be spurred to ordinary crimes as a release for their suppressed needs.

Indeed, those outbreaks of either civil disobedience or disorder we have had in the United States have been not the *cause* of our troubles, but the result of them. They are the outcome of our slowness in solving the problems of poverty, racism, urban blight. Those who fear the spread of social disorder should keep in mind that civil disobedience is the *organized* expression of revolt against against existing evils; it does not create the evils, but rationalizes the natural reactions to them, which otherwise burst out from time to time in sporadic and often ineffectual disorders. Civil disobedience, therefore, by providing an organized outlet for rebellion, may prevent chaotic and uncontrolled reactions. Riots, it must be said, may be useful as barometers showing government its inadequacies, showing the aggrieved the need for organized revolt; but civil disobedience, controlling and focusing rebellious energy, is more effective in bringing positive change.

So far, I have been arguing against the notion that terrible things will happen if people engage in civil disobedience. But it is the *positive* good of civil disobedience that should be stressed. Democracy must improve itself constantly or decay. If citizens maintain a universal repsect for human rights, rather than for law, the society can change fast enough to meet the swift-moving expectations of people in this century. It is *good* for citizens to learn that laws, when they seriously encroach on human rights, should be violated, that some conditions are so intolerable that they may require violations of otherwise reasonable laws (like traffic laws or trespass laws) to dramatize them. If the effect of civil disobedience is to break down in the public's mind the totalitarian notion that laws are absolutely and always to be obeyed, then this is healthy for the growth of democracy.

I am arguing for a civil disobedience measured to the size of the evil it is intended to eliminate. When someone criticized William Lloyd Garrison for his militancy, he replied: "Sir, slavery will not be overthrown without excitement, a most tremendous excitement." Nor will war, nor will racism. Nor will the maldistribution of wealth in the world, nor the monopolization of power in the hands of a few.

We in America are so far removed from our own revolutionary tradition, and the abolitionist tradition, and also from the reality of suffering among other people, that we consider as unpardonable transgressions of law and order what are really mild acts, measured against the existing evils. For students to occupy a university building in protest against that University's long-time policy of pushing black people from their homes while it accumulated enormous wealth—that is a mild action. For black Mississippians to occupy government property in protest against their poverty is a pitifully moderate act. For a young person to burn a draft card is a rather weak form of protest against a government which drops bombs on villages, destroys crops, kills thousands in war.

"It Isn't Nice" *by Malvina Reynolds*

This song, written in 1964, can be a companion piece to Thoreau's essay. How would Thoreau react to the title and its message?

* * *

2. It isn't nice to carry banners
   Or to sit in on the floor,
   Or to shout our cry of Freedom
   At the hotel and the store,
   It isn't nice, it isn't nice,
   You told us once, you told us twice,
   But if that is Freedom's price,
   We don't mind.

3. We have tried negotiations
   And the three-man picket line,
   Mr. Charlie didn't see us
   And he might as well be blind.
   Now our new ways aren't nice
   When we deal with men of ice,
   But if that is Freedom's price,
   We don't mind.

4. How about those years of lynchings
   And the shot in Evers' back?
   Did you say it wasn't proper,
   Did you stand out on the track?
   You were quiet just like mice,
   Now you say we aren't nice,
   But if that is Freedom's price,
   We don't mind.

5. It isn't nice to block the doorway,
   It isn't nice to go to jail,
   There are nicer ways to do it
   But the nice ways always fail.
   It isn't nice, it isn't nice,
   But thanks for your advice,
   Cause if that is Freedom's price,
   We don't mind.

"Statement" *by Bartolomeo Vanzetti*

In the 1920s, Nicola Sacco and Bartolomeo Vanzetti were tried, convicted, and executed for murder and robbery. Many people believe their conviction was not the result of the evidence presented at their trial, but of the men's reputations as radicals. The trial and the pretrial publicity became a vehicle for the airing of this viewpoint. It is ironic that in July 1977, the Governor of Massachusetts set aside a day to commemorate Sacco and Vanzetti. His action then set off a new round of controversy surrounding their execution.

The "statement" by Bartolomeo Vanzetti that follows is taken from Philip Stong's newspaper account of an interview with Vanzetti just before his execution in 1927, six years after the trial.

* * *

If it had not been for these thing, I might have live out my life talking at street corners to scorning men. I might have die, unmarked, unknown, a failure. Now we are not a failure. This is our career and our triumph. Never in our full life can we hope to do such work for tolerance, for joostice, for man's onderstanding of man, as we do now by an accident.

Our words—our lives—our pains—nothing! The taking of our lives—lives of a good shoemaker and a poor fish-peddler—all! That last moment belong to us—that agony is our triumph!

From **Scoundrel Time** *by Lillian Hellman*

The House Committee on Un-American Activities held widely publicized hearings in the 1950s. This arm of the United States government was investigating alleged communist influence in many areas of life, but particularly in the entertainment industry. Lillian Hellman's career as a writer was in jeopardy at this time; nevertheless, she forwarded this letter to the Committee in advance of her appearance at the hearing.

It is interesting to note that years later, Ms. Hellman received a standing ovation at the 1976 Academy Awards presentation from an audience who recognized her singular achievement. This was especially heartening for the many other writers who had been the victims of an unofficial blacklist for not cooperating with the Committee's investigation.

* * *

In April of 1952 I put the Pleasantville farm up for sale, and the shock of that may be the reason I have so little memory, and almost no notes, for the few weeks before my appearance before the Committee. I know, of course, that Rauh wrote a letter that I was to send to the Committee; I didn't like it much because it didn't sound like me. Then I wrote a version, he wrote another, I rewrote him, he rewrote me, and we came out with the version that I quote here.

May 19, 1952

Honorable John S. Wood
Chairman
House Committee on Un-American Activities
Room 226 Old House Office Building
Washington 25, D.C.

Dear Mr. Wood:

As you know, I am under subpoena to appear before your Committee on May 21, 1952.

I am most willing to answer all questions about myself. I have nothing to hide from your Committee and there is nothing in my life of which I am ashamed. I have been advised by counsel that under the Fifth Amendment I have a constitutional privilege to decline to answer any questions about my political opinions, activities and associations, on the grounds of self-incrimination. I do not wish to claim this privilege. I am ready and willing to testify before the representatives of our Government as to my own opinions and my own actions, regardless of any risks or consequences to myself.

But I am advised by counsel that if I answer the Committee's questions about myself, I must also answer questions about other people and that if I refuse to do so, I can be cited for contempt. My counsel tells me that if I answer questions about myself, I will have waived my rights under the Fifth Amendment and could be forced legally to answer questions about others. This is very difficult for a layman to understand. But there is one principle that I do understand: I am not willing, now or in the future, to bring bad trouble to people who, in my past association with them, were completely innocent of any talk or any action that was disloyal or subversive. I do not like subversion or disloyalty in any form and if I had ever seen any I would have considered it my duty to have reported it to the proper authorities. But to hurt innocent people whom I knew many years ago in order to save myself is, to me, inhuman and indecent and dishonorable. I cannot and will not cut my conscience to fit this year's fashions, even though I long ago came to the conclusion that I was not a

LILLIAN HELLMAN. N.Y. PUBLIC LIBRARY, PICTURE COLLECTION.

political person and could have no comfortable place in any political group.

I was raised in an old-fashioned American tradition and there were certain homely things that were taught to me: to try to tell the truth, not to bear false witness, not to harm my neighbor, to be loyal to my country, and so on. In general, I respected these ideals of Christian honor and did as well with them as I knew how. It is my belief that you will agree with these simple rules of human decency and will not expect me to violate the good American tradition from which they spring. I would, therefore, like to come before you and speak of myself.

I am prepared to waive the privilege against self-incrimination and to tell you anything you wish to know about my views or actions if your Committee will agree to refrain from asking me to name other people. If the Committee is unwilling to give me this assurance, I will be forced to plead the privilege of the Fifth Amendment at the hearing.

A reply to this letter would be appreciated.

Sincerely yours,

Lillian Hellman

Topics for Discussion, Research, and Composition

1. a. "Society in every state is a blessing but government even in its best state is a necessary evil." In what way is society a blessing? In what way is government an evil? Why is it a necessary evil?
   b. Your school, too, is run by a form of government. Describe the way in which this "government" is as necessary an evil as Thomas Paine says all governments are.
2. a. Thoreau realized that government is an expedient. How does this compare to Thomas Paine's calling government a necessary evil?
   b. "Let every man make known what kind of government could command his respect and that will be one step toward obtaining it." Canvass members of your family or people in your school or neighborhood. Ask them to explain the ways in which our government can be better.
3. Should the majority rule? What would be the consequences of having a government "in which majorities do not virtually decide right and wrong, but conscience"?
4. How would the author of "It Isn't Nice" respond to the questionnaire in the introduction?
5. a. Howard Zinn refers to the possible dangers of allowing acts of civil disobedience. What are those dangers? How does he show that those fears are groundless?
   b. Was the looting that occurred during the 1977 blackout in New York City civil disobedience or riot? How would Howard Zinn assess this situation? Base your answers on his reply to Abe Fortas.
6. a. Some people believe that "all politicians are crooks." Why are some people so ready to believe the worst about our political system and our politicians? What are you ready to believe and why?
   b. The laws related to financing political campaigns were passed to make it more difficult to influence a politician's vote. How effective are these laws? How does the expense of a political campaign

cause a politician to become potentially obligated to people who may want to take advantage of his or her influence?

c. Comment on this statement: It is better to nominate and elect only wealthy politicians. If they are rich enough, they can't be bought.

7. There have been some plays and movies that deal with the House Committee on Un-American Activities and the writers who faced its investigation. It may be possible for you either to read the scripts or to see them at some time. Look for the following titles: *The Front; The Way We Were; Have You Now or Have You Ever Been.*

3

Civil Rights

I Want What Is Mine! I Demand My Rights!

What are your rights? Is it what the law allows? At one time the law allowed people to own and sell slaves.

What are your rights? Is it to do what everyone else does? At one time (and in some areas today) parents arranged the marriages of their children. To select your own mate whom you loved was considered foolish and perhaps dangerous.

What are your rights? Is it what the community at large feels is right? Prevailing standards in some communities today allow books to be banned and movies to be censored. The law allows someone to sell books in one state and yet be arrested for selling the same books in another state.

What are your rights? Is it to say and to do what you think is right even if everyone else disagrees? And what if what you think is your right to live where you want, for example, conflicts with what other people think is their right not to rent or to sell to you?

What is right and what is a civil right has been open to change and to interpretation. That is why the struggle for civil rights is an ongoing battle. It has largely focused on the rights of black men and women, the rights of men and women of other ethnic groups, and on the rights of all women. However, the civil rights movement will continue to be active as long as people find it necessary to say, "I want what is mine! I demand my rights!"

BLACKS

from **Uncle Tom's Cabin** *by Harriet Beecher Stowe*

People who have not read Uncle Tom's Cabin *probably have many misconceptions about the book because "Uncle Tom" has become a pejorative expression to many people. The real hero of the book is George, whose strength, courage, and independence would make him a leader even today.*

When Abraham Lincoln was introduced to Harriet Beecher Stowe, he reportedly said, "So this is the little lady that started the Civil War." It is no wonder that this is a landmark book. When reading these two excerpts, keep in mind that they were written ten years before the Civil War started. They were truly revolutionary thoughts then and, in some ways, they still are.

* * *

Mr. Wilson, a good-natured but extremely fidgety and cautious old gentleman, ambled up and down the room, appearing, as John Bunyan hath it, "much tumbled up and down in his mind," and divided between his wish to help George, and a certain confused notion of maintaining law and order: so, as he shambled about, he delivered himself as follows:—

"Well, George, I s'pose you're running away,—leaving your lawful master, George,—(I don't wonder at it),—at the same time, I'm sorry, George,—yes, decidedly,—I think I must say that, George,—it's my duty to tell you so."

"Why are you sorry, sir?" said George, calmly.

"Why, to see you, as it were, setting yourself in opposition to the laws of your country."

"My country!" said George, with a strong and bitter emphasis; "what country have I, but the grave,—and I wish to God that I was laid there!"

"Why, George, no,—no,—it won't do; this way of talking is wicked,—unscriptural. George, you've got a hard master,—in fact, he is—well, he conducts himself reprehensibly,—I can't pretend to defend him. But you know how the angel commanded Hagar to return to her mistress, and submit herself under her hand; and the apostle sent back Onesimus to his master."

"Don't quote Bible at me that way, Mr. Wilson," said George, with a flashing eye, "don't! for my wife is a Christian, and I mean to be, if ever I get to where I can; but to quote Bible to a fellow in my circumstances is enough to make him give it up altogether. I appeal to God Almighty,—I'm willing to go with the case to him, and ask him if I do wrong to seek my freedom."

"These feelings are quite natural, George," said the good-natured man, blowing his nose. "Yes, they're natural, but it is my duty not to encourage 'em in you. Yes, my boy, I'm sorry for you, now; it's a bad case,—very bad; but the apostle says. 'Let every one abide in the condition in which he is called.' We must all submit to the indications of Providence, George,—don't you see?"

George stood with his head drawn back, his arms folded tightly over his broad breast, and a bitter smile curling his lips.

"I wonder, Mr. Wilson, if the Indians should come and take you a prisoner away from your wife and children, and want to keep you all your life hoeing corn for them, if you'd think it your duty to abide in the condition in which you were called. I rather think that you'd think the first stray horse you could find an indication of Providence,—shouldn't you?"

The little old gentleman stared with both eyes at this illustration of the case; but, though not much of a reasoner, he had the sense in which some logicians on this particular subject do not excel,—that of saying nothing, where nothing could be said. So, as he stood carefully stroking his umbrella, and folding and patting down all the creases in it, he proceeded on with his exhortations in a general way.

"You see, George, you know, now, I always have stood your friend; and whatever I've said, I've said for your good. Now, here, it seems to me, you're running an awful risk. You can't hope to carry it out. If you're taken, it will e worse with you than ever; they'll only abuse you, and half kill you, and sell you down river."

"Mr. Wilson, I know all this," said George. "I *do* run a risk, but"—he threw open his overcoat, and showed two pistols and a bowie-knife. "There!" he said; "I'm ready for 'em! Down south I never *will* go. No! if it comes to that, I can earn myself at least six feet of free soil,—the first and last I shall ever own in Kentucky!"

"Why, George, this state of mind is awful; it's getting really desperate, George. I'm concerned. Going to break the laws of your country!"

"My country again! Mr. Wilson, *you* have a country; but what country have *I*, or any one like me, born of slave mothers? What laws are there for us? We don't make them,—we don't consent to them,—we have nothing to do with them; all they do for us is to crush us, and keep us down. Haven't I heard your Fourth-of-July speeches? Don't you tell us all, once a year, that governments derive their just power from the consent of the governed? Can't a fellow *think*, that hears such things? Can't he put this and that together, and see what it comes to?"

Mr. Wilson's mind was one of those that may not unaptly be represented by a bale of cotton,—downy, soft, benevolently fuzzy and confused. He really pitied George with all his heart, and had a sort of dim and cloudy pe   neption of the style of feeling that agitated him; but he deemed it his duty to go on talking *good* to him, with infinite pertinacity.

"George, this is bad. I must tell you, you know, as a friend, you'd better not be meddling with such notions; they are bad, George, very bad, for boys in your condition,—very;" and Mr. Wilson sat down to a table, and began nervously chewing the handle of his umbrella.

"See here, now, Mr. Wilson," said George, coming up and seating himself determinately down in front of him; "look at me, now. Don't I sit before you, every wey, just as much a man as you are? Look at my face,—look at my hands,—look at my body," and the young man drew himself up proudly; "why am I *not* a man, as much as anybody? Well, Mr. Wilson, hear what I can tell you. I had a father—one of your Kentucky gentlemen—who didn't think enough of me to keep me from being sold with his dogs and horses, to satisfy the estate, when he died. I saw my mother put up at sheriff's sale, with her seven children. They were sold before her eyes, one by one, all to different masters; and I was the youngest. She came and kneeled down before old Mas'r, and begged him to buy her with me, that she might have at least one child with her; and he kicked her away with his heavy boot. I saw him do it; and the last that I heard was her moans and screams, when I was tied to his horse's neck, to be carried off to his place."

"Well then?"

"My master traded with one of the men, and bought my oldest sister. She was a pious, good girl,—a member of the Baptist Church,—and as handsome as my poor mother had been. She was well brought up, and had good manners. At first, I was glad she was bought, for I had one friend near me. I was soon sorry for it. Sir, I have stood at the door and heard her whipped, when it seemed as if every blow cut into my naked heart, and I couldn't do anything to help her; and she was whipped, sir, for wanting to live a decent Christian life, such as your laws give no slave girl a right to live; and at last I saw her chained with a trader's gang, to be sent to market in Orleans,—sent there for nothing else but that,—and that's the last I know of her. Well, I grew up,—long years and years,—no father, no mother, no sister, not a living soul that cared for me more than a dog; nothing but whipping, scolding, starving. Why, sir, I've been so hungry that I have been glad to take the bones they threw to their dogs; and yet, when I was a little fellow, and laid awake whole nights and cried, it wasn't the hunger, it wasn't the whipping, I cried for. No, sir; it was for *my mother* and *my sisters*,—it was because I hadn't a friend to love me on earth. I never knew what peace or comfort was. I never had a kind word spoken to me till I came to work in your factory. Mr Wilson, you treated me well; you encouraged me to do well, and to learn to read and write, and to try to make something of myself; and God knows how grateful I am for it. Then, sir, I found my wife; you've seen her,—you know how beautiful she is. When I found she loved me, when I married her, I scarcely could believe I was alive, I was so happy; and, sir, she is as good as she is beautiful. But now what? Why, now comes my master, takes me right away from my work, and my friends, and all I like, and grinds me down into the very dirt! And why? Because, he says, I forgot who I was; he says, to teach me that I am only a nigger! After all, and last of all, he comes between me and my wife, and says I shall give her up, and live with another woman. And all this your laws give him power to do, in spite of God or man. Mr. Wilson, look at it! There isn't *one* of all these things, that have broken the hearts of my mother and my sister, and my wife and myself, but your laws allow, and give every man power to do, in Kentucky, and none can say to him nay! Do you call these the laws of *my* country? Sir, I haven't any country, any more than I have any father. But I'm going to have one. I don't want anything of *your* country, except to be let alone,—to go peaceably out of it; and when I get to Canada, where the laws will own me and protect me, *that* shall be my country, and its laws I will obey. But if any man tries to stop me, let him take care, for I am desperate. I'll fight for my liberty to the last breath I breathe. You say your fathers did it; if it was right for them, it is right for me!"

*   *   *

George remained four years at a French university, and, applying himself with an unintermitted zeal, obtained a very thorough education.

Political troubles in France, at last, led the family again to seek an asylum in this country.

George's feelings and views, as an educated man, may be best expressed in a letter to one of his friends.

"I feel somewhat at a loss, as to my future course. True, as you have said to me, I might mingle in the circles of the whites, in this country, my shade of color is so slight, and that of my wife and family scarce perceptible. Well, perhaps, on sufferance, I might. But, to tell you the truth, I have no wish to.

"My sympathies are not for my father's race, but for my mother's. To him I was no more than a fine dog or horse; to my poor heart-broken mother I was a *child*; and, though I never saw her, after the cruel sale that separated us, till she died, yet I *know* she always loved me dearly. I know it by my own heart. When I think of all she suffered, of my own early sufferings, of the distresses and struggles of my heroic wife, of my sister, sold in the New Orleans slave-market,—though I hope to have no unchristian sentiments, yet I may be excused for saying, I have no wish to pass for an American, or to identify myself with them.

"It is with the oppressed, enslaved African race that I cast in my lot; and, if I wished anything, I would wish myself two shades darker, rather than one lighter.

"The desire and yearning of my soul is for an African *nationality.* I want a people that shall have a tangible, separate existence of its own; and where am I to look for it? Not in Hayti; for in Hayti they had nothing to start with. A stream cannot rise above its fountain. The race that formed the character of the Haytiens was a worn-out, effeminate one; and, of course, the subject race will be centuries in rising to anything.

"Where, then, shall I look? On the shores of Africa I see a republic,—a republic formed of picked men, who, by energy and self-educating force, have, in many cases, individually, raised themselves above a condition of slavery. Having gone through a preparatory stage of feebleness, this republic has, at last, become an acknowledged nation on the face of the earth,—acknowledged by both France and England. There it is my wish to go, and find myself a people.

"I am aware, now, that I shall have you all against me; but, before you strike, hear me. During my stay in France, I have followed up, with intense interest, the history of my people in America. I have noted the struggle between abolitionist and colonizationist, and have received some impressions, as a distant spectator, which could never have occurred to me as a participator.

"I grant that this Liberia may have subserved all sorts of purposes, by being played off, in the hands of our oppressors, against us. Doubtless the scheme may have been used, in unjustifiable ways, as a means of retarding our emancipation. But the question to me is, Is there not a God above all man's schemes? May he not have overruled their designs, and founded for us a nation by them?

"In these days, a nation is born in a day. A nation starts, now, with all the great problems of republican life and civilization wrought out to its hand;—it has not to discover, but only to apply. Let us, then, all take hold together, with all our might, and see what we can do with this new enterprise, and the whole splendid continent of Africa opens before us and our children. *Our nation* shall roll the tide of civilization and Christianity along its shores, and plant there mighty republics, that, growing with the rapidity of tropical vegetation, shall be for all coming ages.

"Do you say that I am deserting my enslaved brethren? I think not. If I forget them one hour, one moment of my life, so may God forget me! But, what can I do for them here? Can I break their chains? No, not as an individual; but, let me go and form part of a nation, which shall have a voice in the councils of nations, and then we can speak. A nation has a right to argue, remonstrate, implore, and present the cause of its race,—which an individual has not.

"If Europe ever becomes a grand council of free nations,—as I trust in God it will,—if, there, serfdom, and all unjust and oppressive social inequalities, are done away; and if they, as France and England have done, acknowledge our position,—then, in the great congress of nations, we will make our appeal, and present the cause of our enslaved and suffering race; and it cannot be that free, enlightened America will not then desire to wipe from her escutcheon that bar sinister which disgraces her among nations, and is as truly a curse to her as to the enslaved.

"But, you will tell me, our race have equal rights to mingle in the American republic as the Irishman, the German, and the Swede. Granted, they have. We *ought* to be free to meet and mingle,—to rise by our individual worth, without any consideration of caste or color; and they who deny us this right are false to their own professed principles of human equality. We ought, in particular, to be allowed *here*. We have *more* than the rights of common men;—we have the claim of an injured race for reparation. But, then, *I do not want it*; I want a country, a nation, of my own. I think that the African race has peculiarities, yet to be unfolded in the light of civilization and Christianity, which, if not the same with those of the Anglo-Saxon, may prove to be, morally, of even a higher type.

"To the Anglo-Saxon race has been intrusted the destinies of the world, during its pioneer period of struggle and conflict. To that mission its stern, inflexible, energetic elements were well adapted; but, as a Christian, I look for another era to arise. On its borders I trust we stand; and the throes that now convulse the nations are, to my hope, but the birth-pangs of an hour of universal peace and brotherhood.

"I trust that the development of Africa is to be essentially a Christian one. If not a dominant and commanding race, they are, at least, an affectionate, magnanimous, and forgiving one. Having been called in the furnace of injustice and oppression, they have need to bind closer to their hearts that sublime doctrine of love and forgiveness, through which alone they are to conquer, which it is to be their mission to spread over the continent of Africa.

"In myself, I confess, I am feeble for this,—full half the blood in my veins is the hot and hasty Saxon; but I have an eloquent preacher of the Gospel ever by my side, in the person of my beautiful wife. When I wander, her gentler spirit ever restores me, and keeps before my eyes the Christian calling and mission of our race. As a Christian patriot, as a teacher of Christianity, I go to *my country,*—my chosen, my glorious Africa!—and to her, in my heart, I sometimes apply those splendid words of prophecy: 'Whereas thou hast been forsaken and hated, so that no man went through thee; *I* will make thee an eternal excellence, a joy of many generations!'

"You will call me an enthusiast: you will tell me that I have not well considered what I am undertaking. But I have considered, and counted the cost. I go to *Liberia,* not as to an Elysium of romance, but as to a *field of work.* I expect to work with both hands,—to work *hard;* to work against all sorts of difficulties and discouragements; and to work till I die. This is what I go for; and in this I am quite sure I shall not be disappointed.

"Whatever you may think of my determination, do not divorce me from your confidence; and think that, in whatever I do, I act with a heart wholly given to my people.

"George Harris"

George, with his wife, children, sister, and mother, embarked for Africa, some few weeks after. If we are not mistaken, the world will yet hear from him there.

"Address in Court" *by John Brown*

John Brown is remembered in song and in story. It's sometimes difficult to remember that there really was a John Brown who worked to liberate Southern slaves and who was ultimately hanged after his raid on the United States arsenal in Harpers Ferry, Virginia, in 1859.

* * *

"I have, may it please the court, a few words to say. In the first place, I deny everything but what I have all along admitted—the design on my part to free the slaves. I intended certainly to have made a clean thing of that matter, as I did last winter when I went into Missouri and there took slaves without the snapping of a gun on either side, moved them through the country, and finally left them in Canada. I designed to have done the same thing again on a larger scale. That was all I intended. I never did intend murder, or treason, or the destruction of property, or to excite or incite slaves to rebellion, or to make insurrection.

I have another objection; and that is, it is unjust that I should suffer such a penalty. Had I interfered in the manner which I admit, and which I admit has been fairly proved (for I admire the truthfulness and candor of the greater portion of the witnesses who have testified in this case)—had I so interfered in behalf of the rich, the powerful, the intelligent, the so-called great, or in behalf of any of their friends—either father, mother, brother, sister, wife, or children, or any of that class—and suffered, and sacrificed what I have in this interference, it would have been all right; and every man in this court would have deemed it an act worthy of reward rather than punishment.

This court acknowledges, as I suppose, the validity of the law of God. I see a book kissed here which I suppose to be the Bible, or at least the New Testament. That teaches me that all things whatsoever I would that men should do to me I should do even so to them. It teaches me, further, to "remember them that are in bonds as bound with them." I endeavored to act up to that instruction. I say I am yet too young to understand that God is any respecter of persons. I believe that to have interfered as I have done—as I have always freely admitted I have done—in behalf of His despised poor was not wrong, but right. Now, if it is deemed necessary that I should forfeit my life for the furtherance of the ends of justice, and mingle my blood further with the blood of my children and with the blood of millions in this slave country whose rights are disregarded by wicked, cruel, and unjust enactments—I submit; so let it be done!

Let me say one word further.

I feel entirely satisfied with the treatment I have received on my trial. Considering all the circumstances, it has been more generous than I expected. But I feel no consciousness of guilt. I have stated from the first what was my intention and what was not. I never had any design against the life of any person, nor any disposition to commit treason, or excite slaves to rebel, or make any general insurrection. I never encouraged any man to do so, but always discouraged any idea of that kind.

Let me say also a word in regard to the statements made by some of those connected with me. I hear it has been stated by some of them that I have induced them to join me. But the contrary is true. I do not say this to injure them, but as regretting their weakness. There is not one of them but joined me of his own accord, and the greater part of them at their own expense. A number of them I never saw, and never had a word of conversation with, till the day they came to me; and that was for the purpose I have stated.

Now I have done.

"On Being Crazy" *by W. E. B. DuBois*

W(illiam) E(dward) B(urghardt) Dubois, scholar, editor, and novelist, was born in 1868 and died in 1963. His life spanned the post-Civil War period and Civil Rights movement. This selection was written in 1907 and reveals much about the state of his mind and the consciousness of many white people at that time.

* * *

It was one o'clock and I was hungry. I walked into a restaurant, seated myself, and reached for the bill of fare. My table companion rose.

"Sir," said he, "do you wish to force your company on those who do not want you?"

No, said I, I wish to eat.

"Are you aware, sir, that this is social equality?"

Nothing of the sort, sir, it is hunger—and I ate.

The day's work done, I sought the theatre. As I sank into my seat, the lady shrank and squirmed.

I beg pardon, I said.

"Do you enjoy being where you are not wanted?" she asked coldly.

Oh no, I said.

"Well you are not wanted here."

I was surprised. I fear you are mistaken, I said, I certainly want the music, and I like to think the music wants me to listen to it.

"Usher," said the lady, "this is social equality."

"No, madame," said the usher, "it is the second movement of Beethoven's Fifth Symphony."

After the theatre, I sought the hotel where I had sent my baggage. The clerk scowled.

W.E.B. DUBOIS. COURTESY BETTMAN ARCHIVES.

"What do you want?"

Rest, I said.

"This is a white hotel," he said.

I looked around. Such a color scheme requires a great deal of cleaning, I said, but I don't know that I object.

"We object," said he.

Then why, I began, but he interrupted.

"We don't keep niggers," he said, "we don't want social equality."

Neither do I, I replied gently, I want a bed.

I walked thoughtfully to the train. I'll take a sleeper through Texas. I'm a little bit dissatisfied with this town.

"Can't sell you one."

I only want to hire it, said I, for a couple of nights.

"Can't sell you a sleeper in Texas," he maintained. "They consider that social equality."

I consider it barbarism, I said, and I think I'll walk.

Walking, I met another wayfarer, who immediately walked to the other side of the road, where it was muddy. I asked his reason.

"Niggers is dirty," he said.

So is mud, said I. Moreover, I am not as dirty as you—yet.

"But you're a nigger, ain't you?" he asked.

My grandfather was so called.

"Well then!" he answered triumphantly.

Do you live in the South? I persisted, pleasantly.

"Sure," he growled, "and starve there."

I should think you and the Negroes should get together and vote out starvation.

"We don't let them vote."

We? Why not? I said in surprise.

"Niggers is too ignorant to vote."

But, I said, I am not so ignorant as you.

"But you're a nigger."

Yes, I'm certainly what you mean by that.

"Well then!" he returned, with that curiously inconsequential note of triumph. "Moreover," he said, "I don't want my sister to marry a nigger."

I had not seen his sister, so I merely murmured, let her say no.

"By God, you shan't marry her, even if she said yes."

But—but I don't want to marry her, I answered, a little perturbed at the personal turn.

"Why not!" he yelled, angrier than ever.

Because I'm already married and I rather like my wife.

"Is she a nigger?" he asked suspiciously.

Well, I said again, her grandmother was called that.

"Well then!" he shouted in that oddly illogical way.

I gave up.

Go on, I said, either you are crazy or I am.

"We both are," he said as he trotted along in the mud.

"The Funeral of Martin Luther King, Jr." *by Nikki Giovanni*

Martin Luther King, Jr., was perhaps the first black man to win recognition from both blacks and whites as a national hero. He achieved international recognition when he was awarded the Nobel Peace Prize. His actions involved him in peace marches and sit-ins and sparked the march on Washington that attracted hundreds of thousands of black and white citizens. They gathered to support the civil rights legislation being considered at that time. This man, a believer in nonviolent actions, was assassinated. His death shocked the nation and the world.

* * *

His headstone said
FREE AT LAST, FREE AT LAST
But death is a slave's freedom
We seek the freedom of free men
And the construction of a world
Where Martin Luther King could have lived
and preached non-violence

from **Invisible Man** *by Ralph Ellison*

Whence all this passion toward conformity anyway?—diversity is the word. Let man keep his many parts and you'll have no tyrant states. Why, if they follow this conformity business they'll end up by forcing me, an invisible man, to become white, which is not a color but the lack of one. Must I strive toward colorlessness? But seriously, and without snobbery, think of what the world would lose if that should happen. America is woven of many strands; I would recognize them and let it so remain. It's "winner take nothing" that is the great truth of our country or of any country. Life is to be lived, not controlled; and humanity is won by continuing to play in face of certain defeat. Our fate is to become one, and yet many—This is not prophecy, but description. Thus one of the greatest jokes in the world is the spectacle of the whites busy escaping blackness and becoming blacker every day, and the blacks striving toward whiteness, becoming quite dull and gray. None of us seems to know who he is or where he's going.

Topics for Discussion, Research, and Composition

1. a. Outline and match the arguments used by Mr. Wilson to keep George from leaving and the arguments used by George to show why he must leave.
   b. In his letter, George Harris describes the work he intends to do when he settles in Liberia. Use the resources of your library to learn the details of the birth of Liberia. After learning about the

history and influence of that country, attack this question: To what extent do you think George eventually fulfilled his goal?

2. Mr. Wilson used quotes from the Bible to justify his beliefs. John Brown, too, quotes from the Bible to explain his actions. How has each person either used or misused the Bible?
3. Many groups have had to endure comments similar to the ones used in "On Being Crazy." Show how other minority groups were exposed to variations of these indignities.
4. "But death is a slave's freedom."
"No, if it came to that, I can earn myself at least six feet of free soil—the first and last I shall ever own in Kentucky."
Show how these lines from "The Funeral of Martin Luther King, Jr." and *Uncle Tom's Cabin* are complementary.
5. Investigate the killing of Martin Luther King, Jr. Use your library's microfilm file to read the newspaper accounts of his life and death, and of the continuing controversy over the circumstances of his assassination.

WOMEN

from **The Scarlet Letter** *by Nathaniel Hawthorne*

There have been many steps taken by women on their continuing journey toward full equality in this country, but there's a long way to go. One such step was taken by Hester Prynne in the novel The Scarlet Letter. *As punishment for her crime of adultery she was to wear forever on her dress a large scarlet letter "A." Much is revealed in the manner in which she carried the letter and her self.*

The door of the jail being flung open from within, there appeared, in the first place, like a black shadow emerging into the sunshine, the grim and grisly presence of the town-beadle, with a sword by his side and his staff of office in his hand. This personage prefigured and represented in his aspect the whole dismal severity of the Puritanic code of law, which it was his business to administer in its final and closest application to the offender. Stretching forth the official staff in his left hand, he laid his right upon the shoulder of a young woman, whom he thus drew forward; until, on the threshold of the prison-door, she repelled him, by an action marked with natural dignity and force of character, and stepped into the open air, as if by her own free-will. She bore in her arms a child, a baby of some three months old, who winked and turned aside its little face from the too vivid light of day; because its existence, heretofore, had brought it acquainted only with the gray twilight of a dungeon, or other darksome apartment of the prison.

When the young woman—the mother of this child—stood fully revealed before the crowd, it seemed to be her first impulse to clasp the infant closely to her bosom; not so much by an impulse of motherly affection, as that she might thereby conceal a certain token, which was wrought or fastened into her dress. In a moment, however, wisely judging that one token of her shame would but poorly serve to hide another, she took the baby on her arm, and, with a burning blush, and yet a haughty smile, and a glance that would not be abashed, looked around at her townspeople and neighbours. On the breast of her gown, in fine red cloth, surrounded with an elaborate embroidery and fantastic flourishes of gold thread, appeared the letter A. It was so artistically done, and with so much fertility and gorgeous luxuriance of fancy, that it had all the effect of a last and fitting decoration to the apparel which she wore; and which was of a splendor in accordance with the taste of the age, but greatly beyond what was allowed by the sumptuary regulations of the colony.

The young woman was tall, with a figure of perfect elegance, on a large scale. She had dark and abundant hair, so glossy that it threw off the sunshine with a gleam, and a face which, besides being beautiful from regularity of feature and richness of complexion, had the impressiveness belonging to a marked brow and deep black eyes. She was lady-like too, after the manner of the feminine gentility of those days; characterized by a certain state and dignity, rather than by the delicate, evanescent, and indescribable grace, which is now recognized as its indication. And never had Hester Prynne appeared more lady-like, in the antique interpretation of the term, than as she issued from the prison. Those who had before known her, and had expected to behold her dimmed and obscured by a disastrous cloud, were astonished, and even startled, to perceive how her beauty shone out, and made a halo of the misfortune and ignominy in which she was enveloped. It may be true, that, to a sensitive observer, there was something exquisitely painful in it. Her attire, which, indeed, she had wrought for the occasion, in prison, and had modelled much after her own fancy, seemed to express the attitude of her spirit, the desperate recklessness of her mood, by its wild and picturesque peculiarity. But the point which drew all eyes, and, as it were, transfigured the wearer,—so that both men and women, who had been familiarly acquainted with Hester Prynne, were now impressed as if they beheld her for the first time,—was that SCARLET LETTER, so fantastically embroidered and illuminated upon her bosom. It had the effect of a spell, taking her out of the ordinary relations with humanity, and inclosing her in a sphere by herself.

"She hath good skill at her needle, that's certain," remarked one of the female spectators; "but did ever a woman, before this brazen hussy, contrive such a way of showing it! Why, gossips, what is it but to laugh in the faces of our godly magistrates, and make a pride out of what they, worthy gentlemen, meant for a punishment?"

"It were well," muttered the most iron-visaged of the old dames, "if we stripped Madam Hester's rich gown off her dainty shoulders; and as for the red letter, which she hath stitched so curiously, I'll bestow a rag of mine own rheumatic flannel, to make a fitter one!"

"O, peace, neighbours, peace!" whispered their youngest companion. "Do not let her hear you! Not a stitch in that embroidered letter, but she has felt it in her heart."

The grim beadle now made a gesture with his staff.

"Make way, good people, make way, in the King's name," cried he. "Open a passage; and, I promise ye, Mistress Prynne shall be set where man, woman, and child may have a fair sight of her brave apparel, from this time till an hour past meridian. A blessing on the righteous Colony of the Massachusetts, where iniquity is dragged out into the sunshine! Come along, Madam Hester, and show your scarlet letter in the marketplace!"

A lane was forthwith opened through the crowd of spectators. Preceded by the beadle, and attended by an irregular procession of stern-browed men and unkindly-visaged women, Hester Prynne set forth towards the place appointed for her punishment. A crowd of eager and curious schoolboys, understanding little of the matter in hand, except that it gave them a half-holiday, ran before her progress, turning their heads continually to stare into her face, and at the winking baby in her arms, and at the ignominious letter on her breast. It was no great distance, in those days, from the prison-door to the market-place. Measured by the prisoner's experience, however, it might be reckoned a journey of some length; for, haughty as her demeanour was, she perchance underwent an agony from every footstep of those that thronged to see her, as if her heart had been flung into the street for them all to spurn and trample upon. In our nature, however, there is a provision, alike marvellous and merciful, that the sufferer should never know the intensity of what he endures by its present torture, but chiefly by the pang that rankles after it. With almost a serene deportment, therefore, Hester Prynne passed through this portion of her ordeal, and came to a sort of scaffold, at the western extremity of the market-place. It stood nearly beneath the eaves of Boston's earliest church, and appeared to be a fixture there.

In fact, this scaffold constituted a portion of a penal machine, which now, for two or three generations past, has been merely historical and traditionary among us, but was held, in the old time, to be as effectual an agent in the promotion of good citizenship, as ever was the guillotine among the terrorists of France. It was, in short, the platform of the pillory; and above it rose the framework of that instrument of discipline, so fashioned as to confine the human head in its tight grasp, and thus hold it up to the public gaze. The very ideal of ignominy was embodied and made manifest in this contrivance of wood and iron. There can be no outrage, methinks, against our common nature,—whatever be the delinquencies of the individual,—no outrage more flagrant than to forbid the culprit to hide his face for shame; as it was the essence of this punishment to do. In Hester Prynne's instance, however, as not infrequently in other cases, her sentence bore, that she should stand a certain time upon the platform, but without undergoing that gripe about the neck and confinement of the head, the proneness to which was the most devilish characteristic of this ugly engine. Knowing well her part, she ascended a flight of wooden steps, and was thus displayed to the surrounding multitude, at about the height of a man's shoulders above the street. . . .

. . . [T]he scaffold of the pillory was a point of view that revealed to Hester Prynne the entire track along which she had been treading, since her happy infancy. Standing on that miserable eminence, she saw again her native village, in Old England, and her paternal home; a decayed house of gray stone, with a poverty-stricken aspect, but retaining a half-obliterated shield of arms over the portal, in token of antique gentility. She saw her father's face, with its bald brow, and reverend white beard, that flowed over the old-fashioned Elizabethan ruff; her mother's too, with the look of heedful and anxious love which it always wore in her remembrance, and which, even since her death, had so often laid the impediment of a gentle remonstrance in her daughter's pathway. She saw her own face, glowing with girlish beauty, and illuminating all the interior of the dusky mirror in which she had been wont to gaze at it. There she beheld another countenance, of a man well stricken in years, a pale, thin, scholar-like visage, with eyes dim and bleared by the lamp-light that had served them to pore over many ponderous books. Yet those same bleared optics had a strange, penetrating power, when it was their owner's purpose to read the human soul. This figure of the study and the cloister, as Hester Prynne's womanly fancy failed not to recall, was slightly deformed, with the left shoulder a trifle higher than the right. Next rose before her, in memory's picture-gallery, the intricate and narrow thoroughfares, the tall, gray houses, the huge cathedrals, and the public edifices, ancient in date and quaint in architecture, of a Continental city; where a new life had awaited her, still in connection with the misshapen scholar; a new life, but feeding itself on time-worn materials, like a tuft of green moss on a crumbling wall. Lastly, in lieu of these shifting scenes, came back the rude market-place of the Puritan settlement, with all the townspeople assembled and levelling their stern regards at Hester Prynne,—yes, at herself,—who stood on the scaffold of the pillory, an infant on her arm, and the letter A, in scarlet, fantastically embroidered with gold thread, upon her bosom!

Could it be true? She clutched the child so fiercely to her breast, that it sent forth a cry; she turned her eyes downward at the scarlet letter, and even touched it with her finger, to assure herself that the infant and the shame were real. Yes!—these were her realities,—all else had vanished!

"Keynote to the 1848 Convention" *by Elizabeth Cady Stanton*

N.Y. PUBLIC LIBRARY, PICTURE COLLECTION.

When Elizabeth Cady Stanton delivered this speech to the First Women's Rights Convention on July 19, 1848, she could not have known how long it would be before women would get the right to vote in the United States. Why was the vote withheld from women for so long? Are some of those reasons still at work today as people work to pass the Equal Rights Amendment to the United States Constitution?

* * *

We have met here today to discuss our rights and wrongs, civil and political, and not, as some have supposed, to go into the detail of social life alone. We do not propose to petition the legislature to make our husbands just, generous, and courteous, to seat every man at the head of a cradle, and to clothe every woman in male attire. None of these points, however important they may be considered by leading men, will be touched in this convention. As to their costume, the gentlemen need feel no fear of our imitating that, for we think it in violation of every principle of taste, beauty, and dignity; notwithstanding all the contempt cast upon our loose, flowing garments, we still admire the graceful folds, and consider our costume far more artistic than theirs. Many of the nobler sex seem to agree with us in this opinion, for the bishops, priests, judges, barristers, and lord mayors of the first nation on the globe, and the Pope of Rome, with his cardinals, too, all wear the loose flowing robes, thus tacitly acknowledging that the male attire is neither dignified nor imposing. No, we shall not molest you in your philosophical experiments with stocks, pants, high-heeled boots, and Russian belts. Yours be the glory to discover, by personal experience, how long the kneepan can resist the terrible strapping down which you impose, in how short time the well-developed muscles of the throat can be reduced to mere threads by the constant pressure of the stock, how high the heel of a boot must be to make a short man tall, and how tight the Russian belt may be drawn and yet have wind enough left to sustain life.

But we are assembled to protest against a form of government existing without the consent of the governed—to declare our right to be free as man is free, to be represented in the government which we are taxed to support, to have such disgraceful laws as give man the power to chastise and imprison his wife, to take the wages which she earns, the property which she inherits, and, in case of separation, the children of her love; laws which make her the mere dependent on his bounty. It is to protest against such unjust laws as these that we are assembled today, and to have them, if possible, forever erased from our statute books, deeming them a shame and a disgrace to a Christian republic in the nineteeth century. We have met

To uplift woman's fallen divinity
Upon an even pedestal with man's.

And, strange as it may seem to many, we now demand our right to vote according to the declaration of the government under which we live. This right no one pretends to deny. We need not prove ourselves equal to Daniel Webster to enjoy this privilege, for the ignorant Irishman in the ditch has all the civil rights he has. We need not prove our muscular power equal to this same Irishman to enjoy this privilege, for the most tiny, weak, ill-shaped stripling of twenty-one has all the civil rights of the Irishman. We have no objection to discuss the question of equality, for we feel that the weight of argument lies wholly with us, but we wish the question of equality kept distinct from the question of rights, for the proof of the one does not determine the truth of the other. All white men in this country have the same rights, however they may differ in mind, body, or estate.

The right is ours. The question now is: how shall we get possession of what rightfully belongs to us? We should not feel so sorely grieved if no man who had not attained the full stature of a Webster, Clay, Van Buren, or Gerrit Smith could claim the right of the elective franchise.

But to have drunkards, idiots, horse-racing, rum-selling rowdies, ignorant foreigners, and silly boys fully recognized, while we ourselves are thrust out from all the rights that belong to citizens, it is too grossly insulting to the dignity of woman to be longer quietly submitted to. The right is ours. Have it, we must. Use it, we will. The pens, the tongues, the fortunes, the indomitable wills of many women are already pledged to secure this right. The great truth that no just government can be formed without the consent of the governed we shall echo and re-echo in the ears of the unjust judge, until be continual coming we shall weary him. . . .

There seems now to be a kind of moral stagnation in our midst. Philanthropists have done their utmost to rouse the nation to a sense of its sins. War, slavery, drunkenness, licentiousness, gluttony, have been dragged naked before the people, and all their abominations and deformities fully brought to light, yet with idiotic laugh we hug those monsters to our breasts and rush on to destruction. Our churches are multiplying on all sides, our missionary societies, Sunday schools, and prayer meetings and innumerable charitable and reform organizations are all in operation, but still the tide of vice is swelling, and threatens the destruction of everything, and the battlements of righteousness are weak against the raging elements of sin and death. Verily, the world waits the coming of some new element, some purifying power, some spirit of mercy and love. The voice of woman has been silenced in the state, the church, and the home, but man cannot fulfill his destiny alone, he cannot redeem his race unaided. There are deep and tender chords of sympathy and love in the hearts of the downfallen and oppressed that woman can touch more skillfully than man.

The world has never yet seen a truly great and virtuous nation, because in the degradation of woman the very fountains of life are poisoned at their source. It is vain to look for silver and gold from mines of copper and lead. It is the wise mother that has the wise son. So long as your women are slaves you may throw your colleges and churches to the winds. You can't have scholars and saint so long as your mothers are ground to powder between the upper and nether millstone of tyranny and lust. How seldom, now, is a father's pride gratified, his fond hopes realized, in the budding genius of his son! The wife is degraded, made the mere creature of caprice, and the foolish son is heaviness to his heart. Truly are the sins of the fathers visited upon the children to the third and fourth generation. God, in His wisdom, has so linked the whole human family together that any violence done at one end of the chain is felt throughout its length, and here, too, is the law of restoration, as in woman all have fallen, so in her elevation shall the race be recreated.

"Voices" were the visitors and advisers of Joan of Arc. Do not "voices" come to us daily from the haunts of poverty, sorrow, degradation, and despair, already too long unheeded. Now is the time for the women of this country, if they would save our free institutions, to defend the right, to buckle on the armor that can best resist the keenest weapons of the enemy—contempt and ridicule. The same religious enthusiasm that nerved Joan of Arc to her work nerves us to ours. In every generation God calls some men and women for the utterance of truth, a heroic action, and our work today is the fulfilling of what has long since been foretold by the Prophet—Joel 2:28: "And it shall come to pass afterward, that I will pour out my spirit upon all flesh; and your sons and your daughters shall prophesy." We do not expect our path will be strewn with the flowers of popular applause, but over the thorns of bigotry and prejudice will be our way, and on our banners will beat the dark storm clouds of opposition from those who have entrenched themselves behind the stormy bulwarks of custom and authority, and who have fortified their position by every means, holy and unholy. But we will steadfastly abide the result. Unmoved we will bear it aloft. Undauntedly we will unfurl it to the gale, for we know that the storm cannot rend from it a shred, that the electric flash will but more clearly show to us the glorious words inscribed upon it, "Equality of Rights.". . .

from **Letters** *by Louisa May Alcott*

"Equal pay for equal work" is one facet of the aspirations of the women's rights movement of the 1970s and 1980s. One hundred years earlier, Louisa May Alcott exclaimed that same principle with equal fire. It is not really surprising to read her words; her characters were not really such "little women" after all.

* * *

. . .I believe in the same pay for the same work. Let us hear no more of "woman's sphere" from the State House or the pulpit—no more twaddle about sturdy oaks and clinging vines. Let woman find out her own limitations, but in heaven's name, give her a chance! Let the professions be opened to her. Let fifty years of college education be hers. And then we shall see what she can do!

from **Letters** *by Abigail and John Adams*

There would have been no need for amendments to the Constitution if that document covered the flaws and inequities later amendments sought to rectify. Why were the rights of blacks and women not considered? In these letters of Abigail Adams it is clear that she, among others, recognized the problem and had recognizable goals in mind for her sex.

* * *

Abigail Adams to John Adams

Braintree March 31 1776

—I long to hear that you have declared an independancy—and by the way in the new Code of Laws which I suppose it will be necessary for you to make I desire you would Remember the Ladies, and be more generous and favourable to them than your ancestors. Do not put such unlimited power into the hands of the Husbands. Remember all Men would be tyrants if they could. If perticuliar care and attention is not paid to the Laidies we are determined to foment a Rebelion, and will not hold ourselves bound by any Laws in which we have no voice, or Representation.

That your Sex are Naturally Tyrannical is a Truth so thoroughly established as to admit of no dispute, but such of you as wish to be happy willingly give up the harsh title of Master for the more tender and endearing one of Friend. Why then, not put it out of the power of the vicious and the Lawless to use us with cruelty and indignity with impunity. Men of Sense in all Ages abhor those customs which treat us only as the vassals of your Sex. Regard us then as Beings placed by providence under your protection and in immitation of the Supreem Being make use of that power only for our happiness.

John Adams to Abigail Adams

Ap. 14. 1776

As to Declarations of Independency, be patient. Read our Privateering Laws, and our Commercial Laws. What signifies a Word.

As to your extraordinary Code of Laws, I cannot but laugh. We have been told that our Struggle has loosened the bands of Government every where. That Children and Apprentices were disobedient—that schools and Colledges were grown turbulent—that Indians slighted their Guardians and Negroes grew insolent to their Masters. But your Letter was the first Intimation that another Tribe more numerous and powerfull than all the rest were grown discontented.—This is rather too coarse a Compliment but you are so saucy, I wont blot it out.

Depend upon it, We know better than to repeal our Masculine systems. Altho they are in full Force, you know they are little more than Theory. We dare not exert our Power in its full Latitude. We are obliged to go fair, and softly, and in Practice you know We are the subjects. We have only the Name of Masters, and rather than give up this, which would compleatly subject Us to the Despotism of the Peticoat, I hope General Washington, and all our brave Heroes would fight. I am sure every good Politician would plot, as long as he would against Despotism, Empire, Monarchy, Aristocracy, Oligarchy, or Ochlocracy.

Abigail Adams to Mercy Otis Warren

Braintree April 27 1776

He is very sausy to me in return for a List of Female Grievances which I transmitted to him. I think I will get you to join me in a petition to Congress. I thought it was very probable our wise Statesmen would erect a New Government and form a new code of Laws. I ventured to speak a word in behalf of our Sex, who are rather hardly dealt with by the Laws of England which gives such unlimitted power to the Husband to use his wife Ill.

I requested that our Legislators would consider our case and as all Men of Delicacy and Sentiment are averse to Excercising the power they possess, yet as there is a natural propensity in Humane Nature to domination, I thought the most generous plan was to put it out of the power of the Arbitrary and tyranick to injure us with impunity by Establishing some Laws in our favour upon just and Liberal principals.

I believe I even threatned fomenting a Rebellion in case we were not considerd, and assured him we would not hold ourselves bound by any Laws in which we had neither a voice, nor representation.

In return he tells me he cannot but Laugh at My Extrodonary Code of Laws. That he had heard their Struggle had loosned the bands of Government, that children and apprentices were dissabedient, that Schools and Colledges were grown turbulant, that Indians slighted their Guardians, and Negroes grew insolent to their Masters. But my Letter was the first intimation that another Tribe more numerous and powerfull than all the rest were grown discontented. This is rather too coarse a complement, he adds, but that I am so sausy he wont blot it out.

So I have help'd the Sex abundantly, but I will tell him I have only been making trial of the Disintresstedness of his Virtue, and when weigh'd in the balance have found it wanting.

It would be bad policy to grant us greater power say they since under all the disadvantages we Labour we have the assendancy over their Hearts.

And charm by accepting, by submitting sway.

Abigail Adams to John Adams

B[raintre]e May 7 1776

I can not say that I think you very generous to the Laidies, for whilst you are proclaiming peace and good will to Men, Emancipating all Nations, you insist upon retaining an absolute power over Wives. But you must remember that Arbitrary power is like most other things which are very hard, very liable to be broken—and notwithstanding all your wise Laws and Maxims we have it in our power not only to free ourselves but to subdue our Masters, and without violence throw both your natural and legal authority at our feet—

"Charm by accepting, by submitting sway
Yet have our Humour most when we obey."*

Women's Rights Convention Speech, 1855 *by Lucy Stone*

How many of Lucy Stone's arguments are true today? How much or how little would have to be changed for it to be the speech of a woman arguing at this time for her rights?

* * *

From the first years to which my memory stretches, I have been a disappointed woman. When with my brothers, I reached forth after the sources of knowledge, I was reproved with "It isn't fit for you; it doesn't belong to women." Then there was but one college in the world where women were admitted, and that was in Brazil. I would have found my way there, but by the time I was prepared to go, one was opened in the young State of Ohio—the first in the United States where women and Negroes could enjoy opportunities with white men. I was disappointed

*A rephrasing of Pope's lines:
Charms by accepting, by submitting, sways,
Yet has her humour most, when she obeys.
From *Moral Essays,* Epistle ii, "To Mrs. M. Blount."

when I came to seek a profession worthy an immortal being—every employment was closed to me, except those of the teacher, the seamstress, and the housekeeper. In education, in marriage, in religion, in everything, disappointment is the lot of woman. It shall be the business of my life to deepen this dissappointment in every woman's heart until she bows down to it no longer. I wish that women, instead of being walking show-cases, instead of begging of their fathers and brothers the latest and gayest new bonnet, would ask of them their rights.

The question of Woman's Rights is a practical one. The notion has prevailed that it was only a ephemeral idea; that it was but women claiming the right to smoke cigars in the streets, and to frequent barrooms. Others have supposed it a question of comparative intellect; others still, of sphere. Too much has already been said and written about woman's sphere. Trace all the doctrines to their source and they will be found to have no basis except in the usages and prejudices of the age. This is seen in the fact that what is tolerated in woman in one country is not tolerated in another. In this country women may hold prayer-meetings, etc., but in Mohammedan countries it is written upon their mosques, "Women and dogs, and other impure animals, are not permitted to enter." Wendell Phillips says, "The best and greatest thing one is capable of doing, that is his sphere." . . . Leave women, then, to find their sphere. And do not tell us before we are born even, that our province is to cook dinners, darn stockings, and sew on buttons. We are told woman has all the rights she wants; and even women, I am ashamed to say, tell us so. They mistake the politeness of men for rights—seats, while men stand in this hall to-night, and their adulations; but these are mere courtesies. We want rights. The flour-merchant, the house-builder, and the postman charge us no less on account of our sex; but when we endeavor to earn money to pay all these, then, indeed, we find the difference. Man, if he have energy, may hew out for himself a path where no mortal has ever trod, held back by nothing but what is in himself; the world is all before him. . . . But the same society that drives forth the young man, keeps woman at home—a dependent—working little cats on worsted, and little dogs on punctured paper; but if she goes heartily and bravely to give herself to some worthy purpose, she is out of her sphere and she loses caste. Women working in tailor-shops are paid one-third as much as men. Some one in Philadelphia has stated that women make fine shirts for twelve and a half cents apiece; that no women can make more than nine a week, and the sum thus earned, after deducting rent, fuel, etc., leaves her just three and a half cents a day for bread. Is it a wonder that women are driven to prostitution? Female teachers in New York are paid fifty dollars a year, and for every such situation there are five hundred applicants. . . . The present condition of woman causes a horrible perversion of the marriage relation. It is asked of a lady, "Has she married well?" "Oh, yes, her husband is rich." Woman must marry for a home. . . .

The widening of woman's sphere is to improve her lot. Let us do it, and if the world scoff, let it scoff—if it sneer, let it sneer. . . .

"I 'm Sorry Says the Machine" *by Eve Merriam*

We can find many examples to prove we live in an anonymous and impersonal society. The letters we receive that are printed by a computer and the recorded announcements and messages we hear illustrate devices that cause a loss of personal contact and interaction.

Why are frustration and irritation understandable by-products of such impersonal behavior? How does this poem illustrate this idea?

* * *

I'm sorry says the machine,
Thank you for waiting says the tape recording,
Trying to connect you says the voice in the
vacuum at the end of the line.

I'm sorry that sister is not in working order.
Please verify your brother and try him again.
I'm sorry that mother is out of service.
Thank you for waiting, that father you have
reached is a temporary disconnect.

I'm sorry that landlord is not in working order.
Please verify your neighborhood and try it again.
I'm sorry those repairs are out of service.
Thank you for waiting, that official you have
reached is not reachable at this time.

I'm sorry that water is not in drinking order.
Please verify that sunlight and try it later.
I'm sorry that blue sky is out of service.
Thank you for waiting, those flowers and trees
are permanently disconnected.

I'm sorry that country is not in working order.
I'm sorry that planet is out of service.
Please verify that godhead and try much later.
Thank you for waiting, that universe has been
dis——.

from **"Ernestine Rose"** *by Alberta Eiseman*

What do you do when your father selects your husband for you, if it is the custom of the times? What do you do when you do not love your intended husband? If this is the tradition of your people, what are your rights? What is your future if you refuse?

* * *

Rabbi Potowski could not believe his daughter's words.

"Father, I will not marry him," Ernestine repeated, her black eyes flashing an indignant look.

"Why?" asked the rabbi. "He is a good man, a religious Jew. Is it because he is much older than you are?"

"It is because I do not love him, Father. He is a complete stranger to me."

The rabbi sighed. No other girl in Poland talked of love except his daughter; in 1826 a girl married the man her parents chose. Ernestine was sixteen; most girls her age had been married at least a year, many were mothers. He had made a good match for her, betrothed her to a respectable man, many years older and able to take good care of her. He tried once more.

"But the marriage contract is already signed!"

"I have not signed it, and I will not honor it." Her voice was firm and sure.

In the Jewish community in Piotrków, there was no one else who would defy the rabbi. He was the spiritual head of the community; everyone respected his wisdom and his learning. But Ernestine had followed her own will almost, it seemed, since the day she was born.

At the age of five she had begun to read; soon she was studying the Holy Book, refusing to believe that it was only for boys to study. Girls were supposed to learn to cook and sew. Then came the questions: "How was the universe *really* formed?" or "How did evil begin?"

Rabbi Potowski would answer her as best he could. If he was busy, he would sometimes say "little girls must not ask such questions."

"*Why* must little girls not ask such questions?" That statement disturbed Ernestine most of all. Even as a young child, she could not bear to think that there were questions she must not ask, areas that she must ignore. All through her life she would fight against such thinking.

"I was a rebel at the age of five," she wrote many years later. When she was five or six, her parents and their friends would smile and shake their heads as they recounted her latest headstrong saying. But as she grew older the smiles were replaced by disapproval and alarm. In their close-knit, traditional community there was no room for people who questioned authority. . . .

This was the world in which Ernestine Louise Potowski was born on January 13, 1810. Probably she was given a different name at birth, but there are no records to that effect; Ernestine Louise is the name by which she wished to be known. She came into a world in which men and women born in the Jewish faith spent their entire lives hemmed in by regulations made by others; a world of struggle against oppressive laws and taxes, of poverty and no hope; a world of traditions closely held. All the disputes, conflicts, and troubles of the community were brought to the rabbi for his judgment; his young daughter, with her quick intelligence, listened to people's sorrows and felt them deeply.

For most Polish Jews, religious tradition was worn as a protective mantle, accepted gladly. But Ernestine Louise was not one to accept anything without question. After her mother's death, Rabbi Potowski found the burden of her upbringing ever heavier. He had hoped that marriage and motherhood would help to make her less defiant, but Ernestine would not bend.

She went to see the man to whom her father had betrothed her and asked him to release her from the engagement contract. Angry that anyone would turn him down, he refused. No, he would not return her inheritance, he added. It had been promised him as dowry.

What could Ernestine do? Normally, such a case would come before the rabbi for decision, but the rabbi's mind was made up. She would have to take the case before a Polish court, a step almost unheard of among Piotrków's Jews. It was a frightening decision, the most difficult she had ever had to take. She did not hesitate.

She hired a sleigh and driver and drove through high snows and howling winds for many hours, to the town where the regional tribunal met to hear disputes. All through the long, cold ride she thought about the trial that lay ahead. She would present her own case, she decided. Who else knew the circumstances as well as she? Finally she came before the judges, a young Jewish woman brave enough to stand before a Christian court, seeking the right to choose her own life mate. They were so impressed with her defense that they granted her the right to undo the marriage contract and retain her inheritance.

She was elated by the outcome of the trial, happy that justice had been done. On her way back she decided that she would turn the dowry over to her father: he had always taken good care of her, and she had no need of her own funds.

On her return several days later, she found that the rabbi had made a decision of his own. While she was gone he had taken a wife. Ernestine's new stepmother was barely her own age. Soon the sixteen-year-old bride took over the running of the house; Ernestine felt there was no room for her at home. . . .

It did not take Ernestine long to become known in liberal circles in New York. There were many causes to which she was immediately drawn and a wide choice of meetings to attend. Three years before the Roses reached the United States, a small group of reformers meeting in Philadelphia had founded the American Anti-Slavery Society. They called themselves "abolitionists"; they pleaded, to a largely uncaring nation, the cause of liberty for the Negro slave.

Ernestine had never witnessed slavery at first hand. She had never seen black children torn from their mothers at an auction, never watched the overseer's whip slice across a man's back. Yet she had known enough of human servitude in other forms; within months of her arrival, she made the abolitionist cause her own.

Another crusade that soon took up her energy and time was that of rights for women. In the United States, she found out, women were not much better off than they were in Europe. During the administration of President Andrew Jackson the right to vote had been extended to include most men, if they were white, citizens of the United States, and over the age of twenty-one. Women had no legal rights of their own: they could not sue or be sued; they could not vote, yet they were obligated to pay taxes to help support a government in which they had no say. Before marriage, women were under the protection of their father; after marriage, that of their husband. If the marriage ended in divorce, the husband received custody of the property and of the children. Women were not admitted at most universities; if they ever worked outside the home, it was only because of economic necessity, and then they would be given the jobs with lowest pay.

Man had decreed that woman's world was in the home, "that scene of purest and dearest joy, home is the empire of woman. There she plans, directs, performs . . ." So said the most popular women's magazine of its day, *Godey's Lady's Book.* That recipe for female happiness did not reflect the feelings of Ernestine Rose nor of her husband, who fully shared her aspirations, nor of many American-born women, who had a different vision for themselves.

The very year that Ernestine Rose landed in New York, a resolution was introduced in the legislature of the state to investigate ways of improving the civil and property rights of married women. It was a mild resolution, but it was a start in the direction of upgrading woman's status. As soon as Ernestine read about the bill she drew up a petition in its favor and went from house to house asking other women to sign it. Surely, she thought, women would understand the benefits they would derive from such a law; as she knocked on doors in her neighborhood, the door was usually slammed in her face. If a man came to open, he would say that women had too many rights already and not enough work to do. Wives would echo their husband's words: "Indeed, we have rights enough!" many said.

In five months Ernestine managed to collect five signatures! She must have been discouraged, yet she did not let that stand in her way.

She sent off the petition with five signatures to the legislature in Albany and then set out again to collect more in other parts of the city. She was convinced that by explaining to women their condition, "by holding before them the mirror of facts," she later wrote, she had "roused, to some extent at least, their dormant energies." She believed strongly in "rousing dormant energies." " 'Agitate! Agitate!' " she used to say, "ought to be the motto of every reformer. Agitation is the opposite of stagnation—the one is life, the other, death."

It took twelve years before the bill was passed by the New York legislature, years during which she spoke in its behalf, collected thousands of signatures, and often traveled to Albany to testify about the need for such an act and the necessity to begin to update the status of women. In the state capital the bill aroused immediate opposition. It was argued that to grant married women legal rights separate from their husbands' would cause serious marital conflict and might even shatter the institution of marriage. It was sometimes whispered that such rights might lead women into a life of immorality and perhaps prostitution.

There were manwomen besides Ernestine Rose who mocked such arguments and worked hard for the bill's passage. One of them was Elizabeth Cady Stanton, another was Paulina Wright (later Davis); they befriended the energetic young reformer whose background was so very different from theirs. Together with Lucretia Mott of Philadelphia they became the guiding spirits of the new women's rights movement. . . .

In December 1837 a public meeting was called to find ways to improve the common schools, as public schools were then called. There was intense interest in the subject; five thousand people jammed the church where the gathering was held. A prominent minister from Kentucky, the Reverend Robert Breckenridge, rose to speak. He lamented the fact that out of four and a half million school age children in the United States, almost a million were deprived of education. Presently he left the topic and launched into an angry tirade against those godless people who dared to oppose the institution of slavery and advocated women's rights. "Infidels," he called them in scathing tones.

Ernestine was familiar with that word. Whenever anyone championed an unpopular cause, they were accused of "infidelity." She waited until Breckenridge had completed his speech, then she stood up. "Will the chairman permit me to ask the gentleman who has just closed a question in relation to his remark on infidelity?" she asked.

Everyone turned their head toward the gallery; there stood a young woman in an elegant dress, with her black hair in tight ringlets and her dark eyes calmly facing the chairman. It was unusual for a woman's voice to ring out in a public place; that she should dare to challenge a clergyman was so rare that for a moment everybody sat still. A female voice hissed out the words "Infidel! Infidel!" Then the storm broke. People shouted "Throw her out!" "Drag her outside!" There was hooting and stamping, hissing and cursing. Through it all Ernestine quietly stood, waiting for the noise to die down so she could be recognized by the chair. When order finally returned, the minister replied, "The principles of my Christian religion forbid me to fight with a woman," and sat down, to a round of applause.

Many newspapers reported this exchange, convinced that when a woman dared to challenge the words of a clergyman, and in a church, the world zas truly on the edge of chaos. Yet there were people who applauded her courage and requested that she address their groups. Before long she was much in demand by anti-slavery and women's rights groups, traveling at first within New York State, later all through the North and West and as far south as Kentucky and South Carolina. By mid-century, she was often called "Queen of the Platform."

"I look back to that time," she wrote many years later, "when a stranger, and alone, I went from place to place in the highways and byways, did the work and paid my bills with great pleasure and satisfaction."

She was not deterred by the hostility she often met. Some newspapers criticized her accent and manner of speaking, some went as far as to imply that she was a "foreign propagandist" whose activities were subsidized by "British gold." The Albany *Register* warned that unless "the outpourings of fanaticism and folly of this Polish propagandist" were halted, American institutions would collapse. She replied: "Everyone who ever advanced a new idea, no matter how great and noble, has been subjected to criticism . . . but it is quite certain that no true soul will ever be deterred from the performance of a duty by any criticism. . . ."

She died in Brighton on August 4, 1892, and was buried beside her husband, as she had wished. She had long been ready for her life to end, "if I may call my present inaction life, which I don't," she had written, "for action only is life." "But I have lived," she would say thoughtfully to friends, "I have lived."

Topics for Discussion, Research, and Composition

1. What does the punishment of Hester Prynne indicate about the Puritan's moral code? Why is there no reference to the father of her child? Use the resources of your library to learn the story of Ingrid Bergman. This American actress left the United States in the 1950s in reaction to the public's strong negative feelings about her behavior. Show how the circumstances of her "exile" parallel the situation of Hester Prynne.
2. "A woman's work is never done." Develop this familiar statement into an essay which reflects its original application to the woman as

a homemaker. Develop this statement into a second essay which indicates how it can apply to the work and statements of Elizabeth Cady, Louisa May Alcott, and Lucy Stone, and to the work and statements of the present-day leaders in the fight for equality for women

3. "You've come a long way, Baby!" How valid is that statement? What does the way it's phrased have to say about its validity? How do you anticipate your future to be different from your parents' or your grandparents' lives? How do you anticipate your relationship with your spouse to be different from the relationship of your parents?

4

WAR

Before the Revolution in 1776, those who called for war with England were considered radicals or rebels. Those men who signed the Declaration of Independence were risking their futures by doing so. When John Hancock signed, he did so with that now famous signature written large and bold; in the play *1776,* the author has him saying, "We are about to brave the storm in a skiff made of paper and how it will end God only knows." That document, the Declaration of Independence, was a direct challenge to the established authority of England.

During the following two hundred years, the army had come to represent the established authority of America with the President as Commander-in-Chief. During America's involvement in the war in Vietnam in the 1960s, it was those who chanted, "Hell no, we won't go," who were the radicals, the rebels. That chant grew louder as more and more Americans chose to speak against their country's war policy. Ultimately, one President felt compelled not to seek reelection and his successor felt compelled to end the war.

In 1776, the person who called for war was the rebel; two hundred years later, the person who called for an end to war was the rebel. What insight does this give you about the participation of individuals in their country's war efforts?

from **The Trial of the Catonsville Nine** *by Daniel Berrigan*

Philip and Daniel Berrigan are Catholic priests who were arrested for their anti-war efforts. Their trial gave them a world-wide audience for their point of view. Although found guilty, Daniel Berrigan was able to say, "We agree that this is the greatest day of our lives."

* * *

PHILLIP BERRIGAN. WIDE WORLD PHOTOS.

PHILIP BERRIGAN

I am a member of a family including six boys
All of us were born in Minnesota
My father was railroading out there
and he married my mother   who was a German immigrant
I think perhaps some influence on my life

came from these days
Minnesota was pioneer country
We lived on the Iron Range
Most of the people were Scandinavians   Finlanders
Swedes and Norwegians
I remember my older brothers telling at great length
of the struggles they had
to survive in the bitter winters
We were poor
I remember the depression years very well
I think those years had some bearing
on the inclination my life was to take
I think this is true of my brother Dan as well
and other members of our family
We lived with people
and accepted them as they were
During the depression years I remember my mother
welcoming people from the road
There were many men in those days traveling the roads
impoverished and desperate
Even though we did not have too much to eat
she never refused them
This made an early and deep impression upon us

DEFENSE

Will you indicate what your early education was?

PHILIP BERRIGAN

I come from a devout Catholic family
our early years were more or less stereotyped
All six boys went to parochial school
about two miles away
We had to walk both ways and pack our lunches
We were educated by nuns
in a rather harsh and authoritarian environment
We graduated from a Catholic high school
I went to work and tried
to save a little money to go to college
I was inducted into military service
after one semester of college
I underwent training in the Deep South
first in Georgia and later in Florida
and North Carolina
I was perceptive in a dim sort of way
noticing the conditions of Black people
in the rural areas where we trained

I noticed
and remembered
the dire poverty we encountered
One time when we were out on maneuvers
we happened to be trying out the rations
that would be fed us overseas
The climate was very humid and oppressive
and we were famished
at the end of the day
We came upon some Black people
who were selling whole chickens for $1 apiece
We had some money along
Five or six of us
bought chickens and ravenously ate them
Then a white boy came along
grinned at us   Said we had been eating
not chicken   but buzzard

DEFENSE

Did you experience any of the war in Europe?

PHILIP BERRIGAN

I spent about a month
in the British Isles
I saw the devastation of cities
a result of the great German air raids
Bristol   Coventry   Sheffield   London
I think I should add
in all candor
I was an enthusiastic participant in World War II—
in contrast   of course to my present attitude
which arose because of the influence of people
who have surrounded me

DEFENSE

What happened after your discharge from military service?

PHILIP BERRIGAN

I entered the Society of Saint Joseph
for training
toward the priesthood
I lived with Black seminarians
I learned from them
in a graphic way
what it means to be Black
in this country

DEFENSE

Where did you go after ordination?

PHILIP BERRIGAN

To New Orleans to teach
in a Black high school

DEFENSE

Did you participate in the social struggles then going on in the South?

PROSECUTION

Your honor, how long are we going to go on?

* * *

God forbid we should be twenty years without a rebellion. What country can preserve its liberties if the rulers are not warned from time to time that their people preserve the spirit of resistance?

THOMAS JEFFERSON
"LETTER TO GENERAL WILLIAM S. SMITH
NOVEMBER 13, 1787"

* * *

PHILIP BERRIGAN

Very early in New Orleans
I became deeply involved
in the civil rights' struggle
We did voter registration work
We worked with the poor
in the slums of New Orleans
We tried to provide
some sort of bridge
between the Black and White communities
We tried to attack racism at its roots
We tried to open minds a bit

JUDGE

We are not trying the racial situation in the United States, nor are we trying the high moral character of this witness.

PHILIP BERRIGAN

At any rate
I began to investigate
what was called the Cold War
I began to study
how nuclear weapons were engineered
and gotten ready for "duty"
on both sides

*   *   *

FRANZ

The century might have been a good one, if many had not been watched from time immemorial by the cruel enemy who had sworn to destroy him; that hairless, evil, flesh-eating beast—man himself.

Perhaps there will be no more centuries after ours. Perhaps a bomb will blow out all the lights. Everything will be dead—eyes, judges, time. Night. O tribunal of the night, I have taken the century upon my shoulders and have said: I will answer for it. This day and forever.

SARTRE: THE CONDEMNED OF ALTONA

*   *   *

There was a loosely formed group
of peace people
operating on the campuses
I did some work with them
after President Kennedy's assassination
When the bombing of North Vietnam started
we began a peace organization
We were doing very unsophisticated
and unthreatening things
in those days
We were trying to get a forum on the war
trying to get people to listen
But I remember the fierce opposition
even to this
Anyone who spoke out against Vietnam
was apt to lose his coattails
I lost mine
I was transferred to Baltimore
by my superiors
because of my peace activity
The Catholic community in Newburgh
where I had been teaching
was distraught by what we were doing
I was ordered by my superior to keep silent
But then Pope Paul
spoke at the United Nations
I considered this a mandate
to open my mouth again

DEFENSE

What was the nature of your peace activity in Baltimore?

PHILIP BERRIGAN

We always tried
to gauge our activity
in terms of the reality of the war
We started with prayer vigils
with meals of reconciliation
with a few tentative marches
in downtown Baltimore
We began to demonstrate   at military bases
We went to Fort Myers   Virginia
(Fort Myers is the home
of the Joint Chiefs of Staff)
We tried to contact men
like General Wheeler
and General Johnson
former Chiefs of Staff of the Army
to tell them of our concerns
to sit down with them
citizen to leader
The military were immune
from any citizen influence
They were a law unto themselves
General Wheeler ignored our letters
So we went to his home
and demonstrated outside
We were forced to leave
We came back in a month's time
and were forced out again
The third time   we were forcibly ejected
Apart from these attempts
I also tried continually
to keep in touch with the Congress
I made a proposal to Senator Fulbright
suggesting it might be a good thing
to investigate the war
in light of the moral opinion of the nation
We planned to bring a team
of theologians   to testify
before the Foreign Relations Committee
Fulbright was partial to the idea
but he never had political leverage
particularly from the churches
so of course our idea died aborning.
At Christmas of 1967

I also spent two hours
with Secretary Rusk   I went to his office
with another clergyman
We discussed all aspects of the war
He was very gracious
but he did not tell us anything
he had not said before
and that was not enough for us

DEFENSE

Are there any books that influenced your thinking on the war in Vietnam?

PHILIP BERRIGAN

I was influenced by my reading
on both sides of the question
I have read all the authors
on the Vietnam war
including those who wrote
in support of the war

DEFENSE

I would like to have this book, *In the Name of America,* marked for identification. Father Berrigan, I show you Defendant's Exhibit No. 5. And I ask if you have read this book?

PHILIP BERRIGAN

Yes I have

DEFENSE

Did this book influence your thinking as to the legal aspects of the war in Vietnam?

PHILIP BERRIGAN

Yes it did

DEFENSE

I want to make a formal proffer. The book *In the Name of America* has to do with the reasonableness of the defendant's view.

JUDGE

The government has agreed on the sincerity of his views.

DEFENSE

The government did not agree as to the reasonableness of his views.

JUDGE

In that case, I must question the prosecution. Does the government contend that the reasonableness or unreasonableness of the defendant's view has any bearing on the issue of intent? You had better think that over carefully. . . .

(The prosecuting attorneys consult.)

PROSECUTION

Your honor, we say that a reasonble man could have the defendant's views. . . .

DEFENSE

Your honor, the defense has scored a capital point. This is the first time in a trial of this nature that such an admission has been made by the government. But we shall return to this matter later. . . .

Father Berrigan, I ask you: Did there come a time, then, when you began seriously to consider civil disobedience?

PHILIP BERRIGAN

Yes I came
to the conclusion
that I was in direct line
with American democratic tradition
in choosing civil disobedience
in a serious fashion
There have been times in our history
when in order to get redress
in order to get a voice vox populi
arising from the roots
people have so acted
From the Boston Tea Party
through the abolitionist and anarchist movements
through World War I and World War II
and right on
through the civil rights movement
we have a rich tradition
of civil disobedience

DEFENSE

Now, the action for which you are being tried here was not the first such action you were involved in. To state it briefly: seven months earlier, in October 1967, you along with the defendant Thomas Lewis and two others not present poured blood over Selective Service records in the Baltimore Customs House.

PHILIP BERRIGAN

We were prepared
for the blood pouring
ecause we had practiced civil disobedience
in Virginia
In fact my brother and myself
had practiced civil disobedience for years
by signing complicity statements
in support of draft resisters
So four of us took our own blood
and when the equipment for drawing our blood
broke down we added animal blood
We attempted to anoint these files

with the Christian symbol of life and purification
which is blood

DEFENSE

Will you explain why, with a jail sentence staring you in the face, you felt impelled to act again at Catonsville?

PHILIP BERRIGAN

Neither at the Customs House   nor at Catonsville
do I wish my actions reduced
to a question   of acquittal or conviction
Rather I   and all of us
desire to communicate
with the bench   with the prosecution
with our country
We have already made it clear   our dissent runs counter
to more than the war   which is but one instance
of American power in the world
Latin America is another instance   So is the Near East
This trial is yet another
From those in power we have met
little understanding   much silence
much scorn and punishment
We have been accused of arrogance
But what of the fantastic arrogance   of our leaders
What of their crimes against the people   the poor and powerless
Still no court will try them   no jail will receive them
They live in righteousness   They will die in honor
For them we have one message   for those
in whose manicured hands   the power of the land lies
We say to them
Lead us   Lead us in justice
and there will be no need to break the law
Let the President do   what his predecessors failed to do
Let him obey the rich less   and the people more
Let him think less of the privileged
and more of the poor
Less of America and more of the world
Let lawmakers   judges   and lawyers
think less of the law   more of justice
less of legal ritual   more of human rights
To our bishops and superiors we say
Learn something about the gospel
and something about illegitimate power
When you do   you will liquidate your investments

take a house in the slums   or even
join us in jail
To lawyers we say
Defend draft resisters   ask no fees
insist on justice   risk contempt of court
go to jail with your clients
To the prosecution we say
Refuse to indict
opponents of the war
prefer to resign   practice in private
To Federal judges we say
Give anti-war people   suspended sentences
to work for justice and peace
or resign your posts
You men of power   I also have a dream
Federal Judges   District Attorneys   Marshals
Against the War in Vietnam
You men of power   you have told us
that your system is reformable
Reform it then
and we will help
with all our conviction and energy
in jail or out

*   *   *

PHILIP BERRIGAN

I am saying merely this:

We see no evidence that the institutions of this country, including our own churches, are able to provide the type of change that justice calls for, not only in this country, but around the world.

We believe that this has occurred because law is no longer serving the needs of the people; which is a pretty good definition of morality.

JUDGE

I can understand how you feel. I think the only difference between us is that I believe the institutions can do what you believe they cannot do.

PHILIP BERRIGAN

Our question remains: How much time is left this country, as our casualties inch upward, as Vietnamese casualties mount every day? And nuclear war is staring us in the face. That is the question we are concerned about: man's survival.

JUDGE

I assure you I am concerned about your question, for my grandchildren, as well as for everybody else. It is a serious thing.

GEORGE MISCHE

Change could come if one judge would rule on the war. If one judge would act, the war could not continue as it does.

JUDGE

I think you misunderstand the organization of the United States. One judge ruling on it would not end the war. Each judge must do his best with what comes before him. . . .

DANIEL BERRIGAN

We want to think you, your honor; I speak for the others. But we do not want the edge taken off what we have tried to say, by any implication that we are seeking mercy in this Court. We welcome the rigors of the Court.

Our intention in appearing here after Catonsville was to be useful to the poor of the world, to the Black people of the world and of our country, and to those in our prisons who have no voice.

We do not wish that primary blade of intention to be honed down to no edge at all by a gentleman's agreement, whereby you agree with us and we with you. We do not agree with you, and we thank you.

JUDGE

All right.

DANIEL BERRIGAN

Could we finish with a prayer? Would that be against your wishes? We would like to receite the "Our Father" with our friends.

JUDGE

The Court has no objection whatsoever, and rather welcomes the ideas.

(Whereupon, at this point in the proceedings, those who wished to do so stood and joined in prayer.)

JUDGE

(*After 1½ hours*) I have just received a note from the foreman. The jury has concluded its deliberations and is ready to report its findings. The jury will come in now, and the clerk will take the verdict.

There must be no demonstrations from the audience. If there are, I may clear the room, or I may instruct the marshal to take appropriate action with respect to any recalcitrants.

(Whereupon at this point the jury was brought into the courtroom, and the following proceedings were had.)

THE CLERK

The taking of the verdict in Criminal Action No. 28111, the United States of America against Philip Berrigan, Daniel Berrigan, Thomas Lewis, James Darst, John Hogan, Marjorie Melville, Thomas Melville, George Mische, and Mary Moylan.

Members of the jury, what say you: Is the defendant John Hogan guilty of the matters whereof he stands indicted?

THE FOREMAN

We find John Hogan guilty.

THE CLERK

Members of the jury, what say you: Is the defendant Marjorie Melville guilty of the matters whereof she stands indicted, or not guilty?

THE FOREMAN

We find Marjorie Melville guilty.

THE CLERK

Members of the jury, what say you: Is the defendant Thomas Melville guilty of the matters whereof he stands indicted, or not guilty?

THE FOREMAN

We find Thomas Melville guilty.

THE CLERK

Members of the jury, what say you: Is the defendant George Mische guilty or not guilty of the matters whereof he stands indicted?

THE FOREMAN

We find George Mische guilty.

THE CLERK

Members of the jury, what say you: Is the defendant Mary Moylan guilty of the matters whereof she stands indicted, or not guilty?

THE FOREMAN

We find Mary Moylan guilty.

THE CLERK

Members of the jury, what say you: Is the defendant Philip Berrigan guilty of the matters whereof he stands indicted, or not guilty?

THE FOREMAN

We find Philip Berrigan guilty.

THE CLERK

Members of the jury, what say you: Is the defendant Daniel Berrigan guilty of the matters whereof he stands indicted, or not guilty?

THE FOREMAN

We find Daniel Berrigan guilty.

THE CLERK

Members of the jury, what say you: Is the defendant Thomas Lewis guilty of the matters whereof he stands indicted, or not guilty?

THE FOREMAN

We find Thomas Lewis guilty.

THE CLERK

Members of the jury, what say you: Is the defendant James Darst guilty of the matters whereof he stands indicted, or not guilty?

THE FOREMAN

We find James Darst guilty.

A MEMBER OF THE AUDIENCE

Members of the jury, you have just found Jesus Christ guilty.

(Commotion in court. Similar outbursts from other members of the audience.)

JUDGE

Marshals, clear the courtroom.

(Whereupon, at this point the courtroom was slowly cleared.)

JUDGE

Now, is there anything further that the government or the defendants wish brought to the attention of the court?

DANIEL BERRIGAN

We would simply like to thank the Court and the prosecution. We agree that this is the greatest day of our lives.

*   *   *

Th Verdict

Everything before was a great lie.
Illusion, distemper, the judge's eye
Negro and Jew for rigorists.
The children die
Singing in the furnace. In Hell they say
Heaven is a great lie.
Years, years ago
My mother moves in youth. In her
I move, too, to birth, to youth, to this.
The judge's tic-toc *is time's steel hand*
Summoning
Come priest to the temple. Everything else
Is a great lie. Four walls, home, youth
Truth untried, all all is a great lie.
The truth
The judge shuts in his two eyes
Come Jesuit, the university cannot
No nor the universe, nor murdered Jesus
Imagine. Imagine! Everything before
Was a great lie.
Philip; your freedom, stature
Simplicity, the ghetto where the children
Malinger, die.
Judge Thomsen, strike with a hot hammer
The hour, the truth. The truth has birth
All former truth must die. Everything
Before–faith, hope, love itself
Was a great lie.

DANIEL BERRIGAN

"I Ain't Marchin' Anymore" *by Phil Ochs*

Americans have marched in many wars. In a lifetime, most people can recall at least one period when their country was involved in war. Will there be a time when there will be no more wars for people to march in? What will bring this about?

Oh I marched to the Battle of New Orleans
  at the end of the early British War
The young lads started throwin'
  the young blood started flowin'
But I ain't marchin' anymore

For I killed my share of Injuns
  in a thousand different fights
I was there at the Little Big Horn
I heard many men lyin'
  I saw many more dyin'
But I ain't marchin' anymore

For I stole California from the Mexican lad
Fought in the bloody Civil War
Yes I even killed my brothers
  and so many others
But I ain't marchin' anymore

For I marched to the battles of the German trench
  in a war that was bound to end all wars
Oh I must've killed a million men
  and now they want me back again
But I ain't marchin' anymore

For I flew the final mission
  in the Japanese sky
Set off the mighty mushroom roar
When I saw the cities burnin'
  I knew that I was learnin'
That I ain't marchin' anymore

Now the labor leaders screamin'
  when they close the missile plant
United Fruit screams at the Cuban shore
Call it peace or call it treason
Call it loud or call it reason
But I ain't marchin' anymore
  I ain't marchin' anymore.

"All Quiet" *by David Ignatow*

Bombs were a major war weapon in Vietnam. "Carpet bombing" resulted in the devastation of large areas of the country. Periodically, it was stopped to see if that would bring the opposition to the peace table. This poem was written at the start of one of the bombing pauses over North Vietnam.

How come nobody is being bombed today?
I want to know, being a citizen
of this country and a family man.
You can't take my fate in your hands,
without informing me.
I can blow up a bomb or crush a skull—
whoever started this peace
without advising me
through a news leak
at which I could have voiced a protest,
running my whole family off a cliff.

"Musical Vietnams" *by Bob Allen*

Americans take some comfort from the fact that not one foreign war has been fought on American soil; in fact, not since the Civil War has a war been fought on its soil. Does this mean that American soil is impervious to war?

A polyphonic symphony of napalm bombs
sounds a melody of busted babies
gutted mothers
decapitated men
Harmonizing bombers in azure skies
paint paddies below blood red
bone white
dead blue
The rhythm of clattering M-14s
reacts with local citizens
adding further color
to the local scene
This swinging symphony of sound and sight
is the greatest yet performed by the
Great Society

"But who can really dig that jazz
9000 miles away?"
Don't sweat it man let me clue you in
There is a combo in Watts
and a quartet in Harlem
rehearsing groovy sounds
for a spectacular jazz blast
right in your
back yard

"The Altars in the Street" *by Denise Levertov*

On June 17th, 1966, The New York Times reported that, as part of the Buddhist campaign of passive non-resistance, Viet-Namese children were building altars in the streets of Saigon and Hue, effectively jamming traffic.

Children begin at green dawn nimbly to build
topheavy altars, overweighted with prayers,
thronged each instant more densely

with almost-visible ancestors.
Where tanks have cracked the roadway
the frail altars shake; here a boy

with red stumps for hands steadies a corner,
here one adjusts with his crutch the holy base.
The vast silence of Buddha overtakes

and overrules the oncoming roar
of tragic life that fills alleys and avenues;
it blocks the way of pedicabs, police, convoys.

The hale and maimed together
hurry to construct for the Buddha
a dwelling at each intersection. Each altar

made from whatever stones, sticks, dreams, are at hand,
is a facet of one altar; by noon
the whole city in all its corruption,

all its shed blood the monsoon cannot wash away,
has become a temple,
fragile, insolent, absolute.

from **1776** *by Peter Stone and Sherman Edwards*

Why did the United States need its independence? Why didn't everyone want independence if the reasons for it were so clear?

* * *

HANCOCK: The Chair now declares this Congress a committee-of-the-whole for the purpose of debating Virginia's resolution of independence. Mr. Dickinson.

DICKINSON: Well, now. You've got your way at last, Mr. Adams—the matter may now be discussed. I confess I'm almost relieved. There's a question I've been fairly itching to ask you: Why?

JOHN: Why what, Mr. Dickinson?

DICKINSON: Why independence, Mr. Adams?

JOHN: For the obvious reason that our continued association with Great Britain has grown intolerable.

DICKINSON: To whom, Mr. Adams? To you? Then I suggest you sever your ties immediately. But please be kind enough to leave the rest of us where we are. Personally, I have no objections at all to being part of the greatest empire on earth, to enjoying its protection and sharing its benefits—

JOHN: Benefits? What benefits? Crippling taxes? Cruel repressions? Abolished rights?

DICKINSON: Is that all England means to you, sir? Is that *all* the affection and pride you can muster for the nation that bore you—for the noblest, most civilized nation on the face of this planet? Would you have us forsake Hastings and Magna Carta, Strongbow and Lionhearted, Drake and Marlborough, Tudors, Stuarts, and Plantagenets? For what, sir? Tell me for what? For *you? (He smiles, then turns)* Some men are patriots, like General Washington—some are anarchists, like Mr. Paine—some even are internationalists, like Dr. Franklin. But you, sir, you are merely an *a-gi-ta-tor,* disturbing the peace, creating disorder, endangering the public welfare—and for what? Your petty little personal complaints. Your taxes are too high. Well, sir, so are mine. Come, come, Mr. Adams, if you have grievances—and I'm sure you have—our present system must provide a gentler means of redressing them short of—*(Suddenly his manner changes as he brings his fist down on the desk with a crash)—revolution!! (Wheeling to the Congress)* That's what *he* wants—nothing less will satisfy him! Violence! Rebellion! *Treason!* Now, Mr. Adams, are these the acts of Englishmen?

JOHN: Not Englishmen, Dickinson—Americans!

DICKINSON: *(Again pounding the desk)* No, sir! *Englishmen!!*

FRANKLIN: *(He's been asleep, his chin on his chest; now his eye opens)* Please, Mr. Dickinson—but must you start banging? How is a man to sleep? *(Laughter)*

DICKINSON: Forgive me, Dr. Franklin, but must you start speaking? How is a man to stay awake?

(Laughter).

DICKINSON: We'll promise to be quiet, sir. I'm sure everyone prefers that you remain asleep.

FRANKLIN: If I'm to hear myself called an Englishman, sir, then I assure you I'd prefer I'd remained asleep.

DICKINSON: What's so terrible about being called an Englishman? The English don't seem to mind.

FRANKLIN: Nor would I, were I given the full rights of an Englishman. But to call me one *without* those rights is like calling an ox a bull—he's thankful for the honor but he'd much rather have restored what's rightfully his. *(Laughter,* FRANKLIN *laughing the longest)*

DICKINSON: *(Finally)* When did you first notice they were missing, Sir? *(Laughter)*

DICKINSON: Fortunately, Dr. Franklin, the people of these colonies maintain a higher regard for their mother country.

FRANKLIN: Higher, certainly, than she feels for them. Never was such a valuable possession so stupidly and recklessly managed than this entire continent by the British Crown. Our industry discouraged, our resources pillaged—and, worst of all, our very character stifled. We've spawned a new race here—rougher, simpler, more violent, more enterprising, and less refined. We're a new nationality, Mr. Dickinson—we require a new nation.

DICKINSON: That may be your opinion, Dr. Franklin, but as I said, the people feel quite differently.

JOHN: What do you know about the people, Dickinson? You don't speak for the people; you represent only yourself. And that precious "status quo" you keep imploring the people to preserve for *their* own good is nothing more than the eternal preservation of *your* own property!

DICKINSON: Mr. Adams, you have an annoying talent for making such delightful words as "property" sound quite distasteful. In Heaven's name, what's wrong with property? Perhaps you've forgotten that many of us first came to these shores in order to secure rights to property—and that we hold *those* rights no less dear than the rights you speak of.

JOHN: So safe, so fat, so comfortable in Pennsylvania—

DICKINSON: And what is this independence of yours except the private grievance of Massachusetts? Why, even your own cousin, so busy now with his seditious activities in Boston that he has no time to attend this Congress, is a fugitive with a price on his head!

HANCOCK: Slowly, Mr. Dickinson. I remind you that the same price that covers Sam Adams also covers me—we are wanted together.

DICKINSON: What did you expect? You both dress up like red savages in order to commit piracy against one of His Majesty's ships—an event so embarrassing to your sister colonies that even your good friend Dr. Franklin offered to pay for all that spilt tea from his own pocket!
FRANKLIN: I'm usually able to speak for myself, Mr. Dickinson.
DICKINSON: Then tell me this: what good can come from this radicalism and civil disorder? Where can it lead except to chaos, mob rule, and anarchy? And why in God's name is it always *Boston* that breaks the King's peace? *(To the Congress)* My dear Congress, you must not adopt this evil measure. It is the work of the devil. Leave it where it belongs—in New England.
SHERMAN: Brother Dickinson, New England has been fighting the devil for more than a hundred years.
DICKINSON: And as of now, "Brother" Sherman, the devil has been winning hands down! *(Indicating* JOHN) Why, at this very moment he is sitting here in this Congress! Don't let him deceive you—this proposal is entirely his doing! It may bear Virginia's name, but it reeks of Adams, Adams, and more Adams! Look at him—ready to lead this continent down the fiery path of total destruction!
JOHN: Good God! Why can't you acknowledge what already exists? It has been more than a year since Concord and Lexington. Dammit, man, we're at war right now!
DICKINSON: *You* may be at war—you: Boston and John Adams—but you will never speak for Pennsylvania!
READ: *(Jumping up)* Nor for Delaware!
RODNEY: Mr. Read, you represent only one-third of Delaware!
READ: The sensible third, Mr. Rodney!
MCKEAN: Sit down, y'little roach, or I'll knock y'down!
HANCOCK: Sit down, all three of you! *McNair!!* Do something about these damned flies!
HOPKINS: *McNair!!* Fetch me a rum!
HANCOCK: Get the flies first!
MCNAIR: I've only got two hands!
HANCOCK: *(Mopping his brow)* Christ, it's hot! Please do go on, gentlemen; you're making the only breeze in Philadelphia.
RUTLEDGE: Mr. Adams, perhaps you could clear something up for *me:* after we have achieved independence, who do you propose would govern in South Carolina?
JOHN: The people, of course.
RUTLEDGE: Which people, sir? The people of South Carolina? Or the people of Massachusetts?
HOPKINS: Why don't you admit it, Neddy? You're against independence now, and you always will be.
MCKEAN: Aye!
RUTLEDGE: You refuse to understand us, gentlemen! We desire indepen-

dence, yes—for South Carolina. That is our country. And as such we don't wish it to belong to anyone—not to England, and not to you.
JOHN: We intend to be one nation, Rutledge.
RUTLEDGE: A nation of sovereign states, Mr. Adams, united for our mutual protection, but separate for our individual pursuits. That is what we have understood it to be, and that is what we will support—as soon as *every*one supports it.
WILSON: There you are, Mr. Adams, you must see that we need time to make certain who we are and where we stand in regard to one another—for if we do not determine the nature of the beast before we set it free, it will end by consuming us all.
JOHN: For once in your life, Wilson—take a chance. I say the time is now! It may never come again!
HEWES: Your clock is fast, Mr. Adams. I say we're not yet ripe for independence.
HOPKINS: Not ripe? Hell, we're *rotting* for want of it!
CHASE: Gentlemen, please. What in God's name is the infernal hurry? Why must this question be settled now?
RODNEY: What's wrong with now, Mr. Chase?
CHASE: General Washington is in the field. If he's defeated, as it now appears, we'll be inviting the hangman. But if, by some miracle, he should actually win, we can then declare anything we damn please!
HEWES: The sentiments of North Carolina precisely.
JOHN: Has it ever occurred to either of you that an army needs something to fight for in order *to* win—a cause, a purpose, a flag of its own?
CHASE: Mr. Adams, how can a nation of only two million souls stand up to an empire of ten million? Think of it—*ten million!* How do we *compensate* for that shortage?
FRANKLIN: It's simple, Mr. Chase—increase and multiply!
CHASE: How's that?
JOHN: We will more than compensate—with *spirit!* I tell you there's a spirit out there with the people that's sadly lacking in this Congress!
DICKINSON: Yes, of course—now it's *spirit!* Why didn't I think of that? No army, no navy, no arms, no ammunition, no treasury, no friends—but bless our soul, *spirit!*

Topics for Discussion, Research, and Composition

1. The United States has maintained military services in times of peace as well as in times of war. A peacetime draft for recruits has rarely been used, but there is pressure building to reinstitute one. How would you feel about being drafted in peacetime?
2. Daniel Berrigan: "We agree that this is the greatest day of our lives." How do you account for that statement coming from someone having just been declared guilty and facing jail?

3. Paraphrase what the citizen in David Ignatow's "All Quiet" says. What does he mean? How do you know? How is this a protest poem?
4. Are wars ever justified? Who is to judge if one is justified—the government or the individual citizen? How is the effectiveness of the military influenced by each possible answer? How is the person who refuses to serve in the military to be treated? Should that person be punished or ignored? What effect does each answer have on military effectiveness?
5. How many wars has the speaker of "I Ain't Marchin' Anymore" marched in? Why does he now say that he "ain't marchin' anymore"? Do you believe him? Why or why not?
6. Use the images in "The Altars in the Street" and the details of the introduction to the poem to write a newspaper account of what had happened. Write an editorial for a paper that supported the war and comment on or react to the work of these children. Write another editorial for a paper that opposed the war.
7. Movies are a powerful force that can shape public opinion as well as reflect it. Consult a TV program guide to see if any war movies will soon be shown. After viewing one or two, describe how the films made you feel about that particular war. If possible, watch and compare a movie about World War II with one about the Vietnam War, like "Coming Home," "The Deer Hunter," or "Apocalypse Now."
8. How does a country raise and maintain an army? The United States has used a program on conscription (the draft system) and a program of voluntary enlistment. In 1980, President Carter recommended that Congress restore the draft registration. How can those who do not believe in the draft use "I Ain't Marchin' Anymore" as a theme? What are the implications for the United States if it cannot raise an army?

   Another issue surfaced with the debate on draft registration. Should both men and women be subject to the draft? What are the implications of drafting women? What are the implications for not including women in a draft registration program?

5

ARTS AND SPORTS

Everyone is familiar with the reply of the climber who was asked why he risked his life to scale a mountain: "Because it's there." The artist and the athlete, both, continually try to outdo themselves. They try to hit more home runs, run a faster mile, see the world from different perspectives, create something not previously done. They, more than others, try to extend themselves to explore their physical and creative limits.

The phrase "avant garde" is frequently applied to creative people whose works venture beyond the traditional and the accepted. They, in a way, become rebels in their art. But what happens to these avant garde works? What must the artist and the writer do to maintain a reputation? What are the risks involved?

"Architect" *(Frank Lloyd Wright) by John Dos Passos*

What does an architect do? What does it take to start with a barren property and ultimately see a completed structure? One requirement is vision. Examine this sample of work, the Guggenheim Museum in New York City. What did Frank Lloyd Wright envision as possible architecture that others before him were unable to see?

Examine also the style with which Dos Passos wrote this piece. In what way can this be seen as a collage in words? This is but one section from USA, *which gives us a tapestry of this country.*

* * *

A muggy day in late spring in eighteen-eightyseven a tall youngster of eighteen, with fine eyes and a handsome arrogant way of carrying his

From *The Big Money* by John Dos Passos. Reprinted by permission of Elizabeth Dos Passos.

THE SOLOMON R. GUGGENHEIM MUSEUM, NEW YORK.

head, arrived in Chicago with seven dollars left in his pocket from buying his ticket from Madison with some cash he'd got by pawning Plutarch's *Lives,* a Gibbon's *Decline and Fall of the Roman Empire,* and an old furcollared coat.

Before leaving home to make himself a career in an architect's office (there was no architecture course at Wisconsin to clutter his mind with stale Beaux-Arts drawings), the youngster had seen the dome of the new State Capitol in Madison collapse on account of bad rubblework in the piers, some thieving contractors' skimping materials to save the politicians their rakeoff, and perhaps a trifling but deadly error in the architect's plans;

he never forgot the roar of burst masonry, the flying plaster, the soaring dustcloud, the mashed bodies of the dead and dying being carried out, set faces livid with plasterdust.

Walking round downtown Chicago, crossing and recrossing the bridges over the Chicago River in the jingle and clatter of traffic, the rattle of vans and loaded wagons and the stamping of big drayhorses and the hooting of towboats with barges and the rumbling whistle of lakesteamers waiting for the draw,

he thought of the great continent stretching a thousand miles east and south and north, three thousand miles west, and everywhere, at mineheads, on the shores of newlydredged harbors, along watercourses, at the intersections of railroads, sprouting shacks roundhouses tipples grainelevators stores warehouses tenements, great houses for the wealthy set in broad treeshaded lawns, domed statehouses on hills, hotels churches operahouses auditoriums.

He walked with long eager steps

toward the untrammeled future opening in every direction for a young man who'd kept his hands to his work and his wits sharp to invent.

The same day he landed a job in an architect's office.

Frank Lloyd Wright was the grandson of a Welsh hatter and preacher who'd settled in a rich Wisconsin valley, Spring Valley, and raised a big family of farmers and preachers and schoolteachers there. Wright's father was a preacher too, a restless illadjusted New Englander who studied medicine, preached in a Baptist church in Weymouth, Massachusetts, and then as a Unitarian in the Middle West, taught music, read Sanskrit and finally walked out on his family.

Young Wright was born on his grandfather's farm, went to school in Weymouth and Madison, worked summers on a farm of his uncle's in Wisconsin.

His training in architecture was the reading of Viollet le Duc, the apostle of the thirteenth century and of the pure structural mathematics of Gothic stonemasonry, and the seven years he worked with Louis Sullivan in the office of Adler and Sullivan in Chicago. (It was Louis Sullivan who, after Richardson, invented whatever was invented in nineteenthcentury architecture in America.)

When Frank Lloyd Wright left Sullivan, he had already launched a distinctive style, prairie architecture. In Oak Park he built broad suburban dwellings for rich men that were the first buildings to break the hold on American builders' minds of centuries of pastward routine, of the wornout capital and plinth and pediment dragged through the centuries from the Acropolis, and the jaded traditional stencils of Roman masonry, the halfobliterated Palladian copybooks.

Frank Lloyd Wright was cutting out a new avenue that led toward the swift constructions in glassbricks and steel

foreshadowd today.

Delightedly he reached out for the new materials, steel in tension, glass, concrete, the million new metals and alloys.

The son and grandson of preachers, he became a preacher in blueprints,

projecting constructions in the American future instead of the European past.

Inventor of plans,

plotter of tomorrow's girderwork phrases,

he preaches to the young men coming of age in the time of oppression, cooped up by the plasterboard partitions of finance routine, their lives and plans made poor by feudal levies of parasite money standing astride every process to shake down progress for the cutting of coupons:

The properly citified citizen has become a broker, dealing chiefly in human frailties or the ideas and inventions of others, a puller of levers, a presser of buttons of vicarious power, his by way of machine craft . . . and over beside him and beneath him, even in his heart as he sleeps, is the taximeter of rent, in some form to goad this anxious consumer's unceasing struggle for or against more or less merciful or merciless money increment.

To the young men who spend their days and nights drafting the plans for new *rented aggregates of rented cells upended on hard pavements*,

he preaches

the horizons of his boyhood,

a future that is not the rise of a few points in a hundred selected stocks, or an increase in carloadings, or a multiplication of credit in the bank or a rise in the rate on callmoney,

but a new clean construction, from the ground up, based on uses and needs,

toward the American future instead of toward the painsmeared past of Europe and Asia. Usonia he calls the broad teeming band of this new nation across the enormous continent between Atlantic and Pacific. He preaches a project for Usonia:

It is easy to realize how the complexity of crude utilitarian construction in the mechanical infancy of our growth, like the crude scaffolding for some noble building, did violence to the landscape. . . . The crude purpose of pioneering days has been accomplished. The scaffolding may be taken down and the true work, the culture of a civilization, may appear.

Like the life of many a preacher, prophet, exhorter, Frank Lloyd Wright's life has been stormy. He has raised children, had rows with wives, overstepped boundaries, got into difficulties with the law, divorce-courts, bankruptcy, always the yellow press yapping at his heels, his misfortunes yelled out in headlines in the evening papers: affairs with women, the nightmare horror of the burning of his house in Wisconsin.

By a curious irony

the building that is most completely his is the Imperial Hotel in Tokyo that was one of the few structures to come unharmed through the earthquake of 1923 (the day the cable came telling him that the building had stood saving so many hundreds of lives he writes was one of his happiest days)

and it was reading in German that most Americans first learned of his work.

His life has been full of arrogant projects unaccomplished. (How often does the preacher hear his voice echo back hollow from the empty hall, the draftman watch the dust fuzz over the carefullycontrived plans, the architect see the rolledup blueprints curl yellowing and brittle in the filingcabinet.)

Twice he's rebuilt the house where he works in his grandfather's valley in Wisconsin after fires and disasters that would have smashed most men forever.

He works in Wisconsin,

an erect spare whitehaired man, his sons are architects, apprentices from all over the world come to work with him,

drafting the new city (he calls it Broadacre City).

Near and far are beaten (to imagine the new city you must blot out every ingrained habit of the past, build a nation from the ground up with the new tools). For the architect there are only uses:

the incredible multiplication of functions, strength and tension in metal,

the dynamo, the electric coil, radio, the photoelectric cell, the internalcombustion motor,

glass

concrete;

and needs. (Tell us, doctors of philosophy, what are the needs of a man. At least a man needs to be notjailed notafraid nothungry notcold not without love, not a worker for a power he has never seen

that cares nothing for the uses and needs of a man or a woman or a child.)

Building a building is building the lives of the workers and dwellers in the building.

The buildings determine civilization as the cells in the honeycomb the functions of bees.

Perhaps in spite of himself the arrogant draftsman, the dilettante in concrete, the bohemian artist for wealthy ladies desiring to pay for prominence with the startling elaboration of their homes has been forced by the logic of uses and needs, by the lifelong struggle against the dragging undertow of money in mortmain,

to draft plans that demand for their fulfillment a new life;

only in freedom can we build the Usonian city. His plans are coming to life. His blueprints, as once Walt Whitman's words, stir the young men:—

Frank Lloyd Wright,
patriarch of the new building,
not without honor except in his own country.

* * *

from **My Life** *by Isadora Duncan*

Isadora Duncan is a prime example of an independent person. In this selection you will see the ways in which she expressed this independence at an early age. You will also be able to visualize the style of dancing she pioneered. Her story reflects an interesting weaving of professional and personal styles.

* * *

I went to the public school at the early age of five. I think my mother prevaricated about my age. It was necessary to have some place to leave me. I believe that whatever one is to do in one's after life is clearly expressed as a baby. I was already a dancer and a revolutionist. My mother, who had been baptised and raised in an Irish Catholic family, was a devout Catholic up to the time when she discovered that my father was not that model of perfection she had always thought him to be. She divorced him and left with her four children to face the world. From that time her faith in the Catholic religion revolted violently to definite atheism, and she became a follower of Bob Ingersoll, whose works she used to read to us.

Among other things, she decided that all sentimentality was nonsense, and when I was quite a baby she revealed to us the secret of Santa Claus, with the result that at a school festival for Christmas, when the teacher was distributing candies and cakes and said, "See, children, what Santa Claus has brought you," I rose and solemnly replied, "I don't believe you, there is no such thing as Santa Claus." The teacher was considerably ruffled. "Candies are only for little girls who believe in Santa Claus," she said. "Then I don't want your candy," said I. The teacher unwisely flew into a temper and, to make an example of me, ordered me to come forward and sit on the floor. I came forward, and, turning to the class, I made the first of my famous speeches. "I don't believe lies," I shouted. "My mother told me she is too poor to be Santa Claus; it is only the rich mothers who can pretend to be Santa Claus and give presents."

At this the teacher caught hold of me and endeavoured to sit me down upon the floor, but I stiffened my legs and held on to her, and she only succeeded in hitting my heels against the parquet. After failing in this, she stood me in the corner, but although I stood there, I turned my head over my shoulder and shouted, "There is no Santa Claus, there is no Santa Claus," until finally she was forced to send me home. I went home shouting all the way, "There is no Santa Claus," but I never got over the feeling of the injustice with which I had been treated, deprived of candy and punished for telling the truth. When I recounted this to my mother, saying, "Wasn't I right? There is no Santa Claus, is there?" she replied, "There is no Santa Claus and there is no God, only your own spirit to help you." And that night, as I sat upon the rug at her feet, she read us the lectures of Bob Ingersoll.

It seems to me that the general education a child receives at school is absolutely useless. I remember that in the classroom I was either considered amazingly intelligent and at the head of my class, or quite hopelessly stupid and at the bottom of the class. It all depended on a trick of memory and whether I had taken the trouble to memorise the subject we were given to learn. And I really had not the slightest idea what it was about. Whether I was at the head or the foot of the class, it was all to me a weary time in which I watched the clock until the hand pointed to three, and we were free. My real education came during the evenings when my mother played to us Beethoven, Schumann, Schubert, Mozart, Chopin or read aloud to us from Shakespeare, Shelley, Keats or Burns. These hours were to us enchanted. My mother recited most of the poetry by heart and I, in imitation of her, one day at a school festival, at the age of six, electrified my audience by reciting William Lytle's "Anthony to Cleopatra":

> "I am dying, Egypt, dying!
> Ebbs the crimson life-tide fast."

On another occasion when the teacher required of each pupil to write the history of their lives, my story ran somewhat in this wise:

"When I was five we had a cottage on 23rd Street. Failing to pay the rent, we could not remain there but moved to 17th Street, and in a short time, as funds were low, the landlord objected, so we moved to 22nd Street, where we were not allowed to live peacefully but were moved to 10th Street."

The history continued in this way, with an infinite number of removals. When I rose to read it to the school, the teacher became very angry. She thought I was playing a bad joke, and I was sent to the principal, who sent for my mother. When my poor mother read the paper she burst into tears and vowed that it was only too true. Such was our nomadic existence.

I hope that schools have changed since I was a little girl. My memory of the teaching of the public schools is that it showed a brutal imcomprehension of children. I also remember the misery of trying to sit still on a hard bench with an empty stomach, or cold feet in wet shoes. The teacher appeared to me to be an inhuman monster who was there to torture us. And of these sufferings children will never speak.

I can never remember suffering from our poverty at home, where we took it as a matter of course; it was only at school that I suffered. To a proud and sensitive child the public school system, as I remember it, was as humiliating as a penitentiary. I was always in revolt against it.

When I was about six years old, my mother came home one day and found that I had collected half a dozen babies of the neighbourhood—all of them too young to walk—and had them sitting before me on the floor while I was teaching them to wave their arms. When she asked the explanation of this, I informed her that it was my school of the dance. She was amused, and placing herself at the piano, she began to play for me. This school continued and became very popular. Later on, little girls of the neighbourhood came and their parents paid me a small sum to teach them. This was the beginning of what afterwards proved a very lucrative occupation.

When I was ten years old the classes were so large that I informed my mother that it was useless for me to go to school any more, as it was only a waste of time when I could be making money, which I considered far more important. I put up my hair on the top of my head and said that I was sixteen. As I was very tall for my age every one believed me. My sister Elizabeth, who was brought up by our grandmother, afterwards came to live with us and joined in the teaching of these classes. We became in great demand and taught in many houses of the wealthiest people in San Francisco.

* * *

From her earliest childhood my aunt Augusta had been crushed by this Puritan spirit. Her beauty, her spontaneity, her glorious voice were all annihilated. What was it that made men at that time exclaim, "I would rather see my daughter dead than on the stage"? It is almost impossible to understand this feeling nowadays, when great actors and actresses are admitted to the most exclusive circles.

I suppose it was due to our Irish blood that we children were always in revolt against this Puritanical tyranny.

One of the first effects of our removal to the large house my father gave us, was the opening of my brother Augustin's theatre in the barn. I remember he cut a piece out of the fur rug in the parlour to use as a beard for Rip Van Winkle, whom he impersonated in so realistic a manner that I burst into tears, as I watched him from a cracker box in the audience. We were all very emotional and refused to be repressed.

* * *

When I hear fathers of families saying they are working to leave a lot of money for their childeren, I wonder if they realise that by so doing they are taking all the spirit of adventure from the lives of those children. For every dollar they leave them makes them so much the weaker. The finest inheritance you can give to a child is to allow it to make its own way, completely on its own feet. Our teaching led my sister (and me) into the richest houses in San Francisco. I did not envy these rich children; on the contrary, I pitied them. I was amazed at the smallness and stupidity of their lives, and, in comparison to these children of millionaires, I seemed to be a thousand times richer in everything that made life worth while.

Our fame as teachers increased. We called it a new system of dancing, but in reality there was no system. I followed my fantasy and improvised, teaching any pretty thing that came into my head. One of my first dances was Longfellow's poem, "I shot an arrow into the air." I used to recite the poem and teach the children to follow its meaning in gesture and movement. In the evenings my mother played to us while I composed dances. A dear old lady friend who came to spend the evening with us very often, and who had lived in Vienna, said I reminded her of Fanny Elssler, and she would recount to us the triumphs of Fanny Elssler. "Isadora will be a second Fanny Elssler," she would say, and this incited me to ambitious dreams. She told my mother to take me to a famous ballet teacher in San Francisco, but his lessons did not please me. When the teacher told me to stand on my toes I asked him why, and when he replied ("Because it is beautiful"), I said that it was ugly and against nature and after the third lesson I left his class never to return. The stiff and commonplace gymnastics which he called dancing only disturbed my dream. I dreamed of a different dance. I did not know just what it would be, but I was feeling out towards an invisible world into which I divined I might enter if I found the key. My art was already in me when I was a little girl, and it was owing to the heroic and adventurous spirit of my mother that it was not stifled. I believe that whatever the child is going to do in life should be begun when it is very young. I wonder how many parents realise that by the so-called education they are giving their children, they are only driving them into the commonplace, and depriving them of any chance of doing anything beautiful or original. But I suppose this must be so, or who would supply us with the thousands of shop and bank clerks, etc., who seem to be necessary for organised civilised life.

* * *

But the summer began to wane and we were absolutely without funds. I decided that there was nothing to be hoped for in Chicago and that we must leave for New York. But how? One day I read in the paper that the great Augustin Daly and his company, with Ada Rehan as star, were in town. I decided that I must see this great man who had the reputation of being the most art-loving and aesthetic theatre manager of

America. I stood many afternoons and evenings at the stage door of the theatre, sending in my name over and over again with the petition to see Augustin Daly. I was told that he was much too busy and that I must see his under-manager. But this I refused, saying that I must see Augustin Daly himself on a very important matter. At last, one evening, at dusk, I was admitted into the presence of the potentate. Augustin Daly was a remarkably fine-looking man, but towards strangers he knew how to assume an absolutely ferocious expression. I was frightened, but mustered up courage and delivered a long and extraordinary speech.

"I have a great idea to put before you, Mr. Daly, and you are probably the only man in this country who can understand it. I have discovered the dance. I have discovered the art which has been lost for two thousand years. You are a supreme theatre artist, but there is one thing lacking in your theatre which made the old Greek theatre great, and this is the art of the dance—the tragic chorus. Without this it is a head and body without legs to carry it on. I bring you the dance. I bring you the idea that is going to revolutionise our entire epoch. Where have I discovered it? By the Pacific Ocean, by the waving pine-forests of Sierra Nevada. I have seen the ideal figure of youthful America dancing over the top of the Rockies. The supreme poet of our country is Walt Whitman. I have discovered the dance that is worthy of the poem of Walt Whitman. I am indeed the spiritual daughter of Walt Whitman. For the children of America I will create a new dance that will express America. I bring to your theatre the vital soul that it lacks, the soul of the dancer. For you know," I continued, trying not to heed the great manager's impatient interruption ("That's quite enough! That's *quite* enough!"), "for you know," I continued, raising my voice, "that the birth of the theatre was the dance, that the first actor was the dancer. He danced and sang. That was the birth of the tragedy, and until the dancer in all his spontaneous great art returns to the theatre, your theatre will not live in its true expression!"

"The Pop Sculptor" *by Art Buchwald*

Art Buchwald reflects the attitude of many people toward pop art.

Many people who have looked at such contemporary art have exclaimed, "You call this junk art? Why, anyone can do that." Why is the creator of such art works praised and highly paid?

Andy Warhol is one artist whose works have elicited such comments from the public. They look at his Campbell soup can paintings and wonder why they are hanging in museums and not in supermarkets. By using such material for his work, has Andy Warhol extended our vision? How?

One day the Canadian authorities refused to allow 80 wooden crates, which looked like cartons of Brillo soap pads, Kellogg's corn flakes, and Mott's apple juice, to go through customs as works of art. The cartons, painted by American pop artist Andy Warhol, were not, said the Canadians, works of art but merchandise, and subject to $4,000 duty.

I think the Canadians are all wet. A few days after the incident in Canada, I went down to the supermarket to buy some groceries for my wife. On the way home I stopped in at an art gallery where they were holding a pop art exhibit. Unfortunately, the carton of groceries got heavy, and I left them on the floor.

Then, being so moved by what I saw, I left the gallery and went home.

"Where are the groceries?" my wife demanded.

"Oh, my gosh," I cried, "I left them at the art gallery."

"Well, you'd better get them if you want any supper tonight."

I rushed back to the gallery, but I was too late. The groceries had been awarded first prize in the show.

"We've been looking all over for you," the gallery owner said. "Why didn't you sign your work of art?"

"It's not a work of art. It's my dinner for tonight."

The gallery roared with appreciative laughter. "He's not only a great sculptor, but he has humor as well," a judge said.

"You can see that in his work," another judge added. "Notice how the bottle of Heinz catsup is leaning against the can of Campbell's pork and beans."

"I'll never know how he was inspired to put the Ritz crackers on top of the can of Crisco," a lady said to her escort.

"It's pure genius," the escort replied. "Notice the way the Del Monte can of peaches is lying on its side. Even Warhol wouldn't have gone that far."

"I think the thing that really won the prize for him was the manner in which he crushed the Sara Lee cheesecake on the bottom of the box."

"It makes Picasso look sick."

"Look," I said, "I'm very grateful for all these honors, but my wife is waiting for ththis stuff and I have to get it home."

"Get it home?" the gallery owner said in amazement. "I've just sold it to that couple over there for $1,500."

"The groceries cost me only $18," I replied.

"It isn't the groceries. It's what you did with them. You have managed to put more meaning into a box of Rinso than Rodin put into 'The

Thinker.' Nobody will ever be able to look at a can of Franco-American spaghetti without thinking of you. You have said with this bag of groceries, in one evening, what Rembrandt tried to say in 1,000 paintings."

I blushed modestly and accepted his check. That night I took my wife out to dinner, and the next day I went back to the supermarket and bought another bag of groceries, much more expensive than the previous ones, which I immediately took to the gallery.

But the reviews were lousy. "Success has gone to his head," said Washington's leading art critics. "Where once he was able to produce simple jars of cat food and peanut butter in a wild, reckless, I-don't-give-a-damn-manner, he is now serving up elegant cans of mushrooms and mock turtle soup. The famous touch is gone and all that is left is a hodgepodge of tasteless groceries."

"VTR (videoteleravings)" *by Darrell Perry*

Darrell Perry was a student at Susan E. Wagner High School in Staten Island, NY, when he wrote the following:

```
TVTVTVTVTVTVTVTVTVTVTVTVTVTVTVTVTVTVTVTVTVTVTV
TVTVveni, vidi, vici.video.vi/deo.vid/eo..TVTV
TVTVicanseegod.videity.seegods.vidi.(T(VD)TVTV
TVTV(T(VD)visionarysyphilis.deo.gloria....TVTV
TVTVinexcelsisvideo.videomnipotenti.gloriaTVTV
TVTVmagnacumvideo.gloriainneo-deo.neo.deo.TVTV
TVTVvidi.video.v/ideo.videocracy.ruledbytheVTV
TVTVtubes&glasslenses.ego;id,vid.v(id)eo..TVTV
TVTVnewcranialdepartmentcreatedfortheaccomTVTV
TVTVadationofthenewgod.videosyncrasy.videoTVTV
TVTVvideanarchy.totalvisioncontrol.videityTVTV
TVTVneo-deo!gloria!videomnipotenti!avevideo!TV
TVTVTVTVTVTVTVTVTVTVTVTVTVTVTVTVTVTVTVTVTVTVTV
```

from **Zanballer** *by R. R. Knudson*

The following scene between Zan and the principal was one the author remembered from her own student days. Do you find it hard to believe that people can be treated as role types and not as individuals? In what other areas of life do we find that this is still true?

As the result of a federal ban on discrimination on the basis of sex in the educational programs and activities of a school, funds must be disbursed to teams on an equitable basis. The law has now recognized the legitimate request of female athletes to be encouraged and their teams to be funded.

Why did it take action by the federal government to bring about a policy that appears to be so fair and logical? What were the reasons for the obstacles placed in the way of women who wanted to participate in sports programs?

* * *

"Zan Hagen."

"Your grade and section?"

"8-3. May I please see Mr. Manfred?" A few truants shuffled positions on the bench, looking up at the urgency in my tone. The secretary reached over to answer the phone. After a few hurried "Nos" she came back to me.

"Mr. Manfred is very busy," she said, giving me what she probably hoped to be a discouraging look. "Maybe Monday after school . . ."

"I must see him today. Now."

"Where are you supposed to be this period?"

"At lunch," I lied, knowing she'd send me to history if she knew the truth. I started toward his door, giving the gate of the outer office a businesslike thwam.

"Now just a minute. Where do you think you're going?" She moved to place herself between me and Manfred's office door. I kept walking.

Just then a short bald man emerged from the principal's office.

"Oh, Mr. Manfred, this girl wants to see you."

"Not now. I'm on the phone with the contractor." The secretary looked triumphant. My ears perked up.

"The gym contractor?" I asked. "That's what I want to see him about." He took papers from a desk, turned, and went back into his sanctuary. "Sir, that's what I want to see you about. The gym." I followed him.

He mumbled a few numbers into the phone, then, "March will be fine," and "No, there's no hurry," and hung up.

"Sir, March will not be fine. We need that gym now, today." He seemed at last to notice me. His secretary remained in the doorway.

"That's all right, Gladys. I will manage this girl." She stepped back into the outer office, leaving the door ajar. A long shadow on Mr. Manfred's rug told me she lurked just outside. What am I in for now? He sat there examining me with narrow eyes while I checked out his walls. Behind his desk,a case of trophies gleamed under indirect lighting. State twirling champion Lurleen Dewey held a prominent position on the center shelf next to First Prize, Fife and Drum Corps. Four Southern States Speedball Tournament cups were mixed among Majorette-of-the-year Citations to Ruby Jean Twilley. The bottom shelf, crowded with debate-club trophies and Yell Queen blue ribbons, looked junky. I strained to read inscriptions while Manfred straightened the coffee cups on his desk. Where are his books, I wondered, making a mental note to tell Rinehart that his principal, the school's intellectual leader, had only one book in his office—the Arlington County phone book.

So now the scene is set. Friday afternoon. Outside: rain, thunder, lightning, and mud. Inside: a wet co-ed in huge, bookless office. Across a tidy desk baldy looks up and says, "Take a chair. Now what's all this about the gym?"

ZAN: Sir, was that the contractor you spoke to?

MANFRED: It's none of your business, but yes.

ZAN: And you told him there's no hurry about fixing the floor?

MANFRED: Of course I did. The gym needs a complete rebuilding, from the foundations up. A big job. Takes time.

ZAN: But sir, basketball practice was supposed to begin next week.

MANFRED: And indeed it will. The boys' team is to be bused daily to the YMCA over in Clarendon.

ZAN: The boys? What about our team. We hoped to play in the *Herald* Tournament this spring. We almost made it last year. Please sir, we need a place to practice.

MANFRED: Say, now I know who you are. You're that crazy little girl who raised such a ruckus with the builders yesterday. I heard about your antics, believe me. Screaming and kicking. Not very ladylike. You forgot your shirtwaist, too, didn't you. Have you no shame?

ZAN: But sir, we were supposed to have intramural play-offs yesterday. And next week basketball practice . . .

MANFRED: Yes, yes. But I felt this to be the right time for repairs. And so did the contractor. The "Y" gym has been made available for practice and the boys will play their games away. I've heard that Lee's a strong team on the enemy's court. A real whiz-bang road show. That so?

ZAN: But sir, what's to become of girls' sports without a gym for the season? We don't even have a field to play on. The boys have it for football.

[*Enter secretary who hands Mr. Manfred a manilla folder. She exits. Mr. Manfred scans contents.*]

MANFRED: Now then, Suzanne. I see here that you are fourteen, almost fifteen. Fourteen years old. A young woman.

ZAN: My name is Zan.

MANFRED: I prefer your given name, Suzanne. Softer, more feminine. Yes, Suzanne, you're becoming a lady now. You should cast aside silly ball games and turn to less aggressive, less tomboyish pursuits.

ZAN: Like what . . . sir?

MANFRED: Well, dear, if you must be a sports fan, why not join the cheerleaders. Classy costumes, a few gentle leaps. Stir up the crowds to cheer for our fighting boys. You'd get to shout into that nifty new electric megaphone.

ZAN: Wear those stupid pleated skirts? Feh! I hate maroon. Besides, cheerleaders don't win anything. They don't score points. They waste their energy.

MANFRED: Twirling lighted torches. That should be exciting enough for you, eh? You'd be peaches and cream as a majorette. Running onto the field waving a gold baton. High-stepping all over the end zones. Like a real live fashion model. I can hear the music now. Lee's Golden Girl!

ZAN: Phoney nonsense. I want to play ball. I like to win.

MANFRED: Competition, that seems to be your drive. Well, then, Suzanne, we have proper ways for a young lady to excel. I note here in your record such high marks in English. Did you know that the county spelling bee comes along next month? Suzanne Hagen, Arlington County Spelling Queen. Oh, your school would gain such publicity from that! I shall place your trophy high on that very top shelf. In your years remaining at Lee you could retire that trophy to a permanent niche right beside me.

ZAN: To stand forever between the Pillsbury Baking Princess and the Embroiderer-of-the-Year. Oh, no you don't. I want to play ball.

MANFRED: Say, you'd look mighty cute in a snappy band costume. You'd get your picture in the *Herald.* Sequins sparkling. Furry tassels blowing in the wind. White boots dancing . . .

ZAN: Dancing is my utter worst thing. And sequins itch. Besides, I can't play an instrument.

MANFRED: Never mind that. Any fool can bang a drum. . . .

ZAN: They never give girls the drum. We always have to play the glockenspiel.

MANFRED: Then bang a glockenspiel. You even have time left this season to learn the formations. Tricky things, those marching formations. But according to the I.Q. score recorded here, you can do it. I have every confidence that you'll soon be spelling out "Let's Go, Generals" with the best of them.

ZAN: Listen, Mr. Manfred, the only formation I'd march in would have to spell out, "Give the Lee girls a gym." Otherwise that's all drivel. No, I won't march.

MANFRED: Or spell?

ZAN: Or spell!

MANFRED: Or twirl?

ZAN: Or twirl!

MANFRED: Or cheer?

ZAN: Or cheer!

MANFRED: Or . . .?

ZAN: Or play the Sousaphone. Or try out for the pep society. Or sing in the fall follies. Or join the projectionists' club. Or run for secretary of the student body. Or enlist in the Future Cosmetologists of America. Or change my name.

MANFRED: Now, now . . .

ZAN: And I will not dance!

MANFRED: Hmmmmmm. These psychological tests here indicate such a stubborn streak. You've proved to me that your first-grade measurements are correct. I feel I can be of no further help to you today.

ZAN: But Mr. Manfred . . .

MANFRED: Hmmmmmm. I see from the schedule that you're supposed to go to physical education in just a few minutes. Am I correct? My secretary will show you out.

ZAN: Come to that, where will our gym class meet and what will we be doing all period?

MANFRED: Hmmmm. You'll soon find out, but I will tell you that I've arranged for the girls to have Lee's very largest room, except for the gymnasium which, as you know, is undergoing substantial changes—for the better.

ZAN: Room 324?

MANFRED: Good-bye, Suzanne. Come in for a fatherly chat any time. Gladys, show this obstinate young lady to the door so she won't be late to class. And make an appointment for another photograph for her cumulative record. This ugly one in a sweatshirt is most unfeminine.

Some father, I thought. Some help. I'm doomed. I slunk off to find room 324.

"I'm Free to Be Who I Want" *by Robert Lipsyte*

Muhammad Ali knocked the sports world for a loop. Sports hereos were supposed to be model citizens, an inspiration to the youth of America. Ali was drafted and refused to be inducted into the army. What kind of behavior was this for the heavyweight champion of the world? What could or should have been done about it?

* * *

Two days before he refused to step forward in an Army induction center, an act that would have transformed him into Private Cassius Clay, Muhammad Ali sat in a Chicago motel coffee shop and moodily watched Lake Michigan roil beneath an April storm. Someone asked him why he didn't skip the country.

PHOTOS BY BRAXTON. © SAMUEL J. BRAXTON 1981.

"You serious?" He shook his head slowly. "I got to stay here and lead my people to the right man—Elijah Muhammad."

His tone was so absolute that a breakfast companion felt compelled to justify the question. Hadn't Ali talked about "some cracker soldier so poisoned with prejudice he'd kill me and think he was doing the country a favor"?

Ali kept shaking his head. "Every day, they die in Vietnam for nothing. I might as well die right here for something."

There was very little humor in him that day since the audience was small and somber, and the situation was not one he controlled. Ali has a narrow wit. When someone commented on his English-cut suit, Ali proudly showed the label of a New York custom tailor who also, he said, made clothes for George Hamilton, the actor. There were dry, snide chuckles at the table, but Ali merely mumbled, "I ain't the kind to point a finger at nobody else."

Someone asked him why he didn't just play the game, go into the Army and give exhibitions and teach physical training like all the other major athletes?

He leaned across the table, his eyes suddenly bright, and he spoke with great firmness: "What can you give me, America, for turning down my religion? How can I lose for standing up for Islam when presidents and princes invite me to their countries, when little people all over the East and Africa stop me in the street and say, 'Eat at my house, brother. Be an honor if you stay with us, brother'?

"You want me to give up all this love, America? You want me to do what the white man says and go fight a war against some people I don't know nothing about—get some freedom for some other people when my own people can't get theirs here?

"You want me to be so scared of the white man I'll go and get two arms shot off and 10 medals so you can give me a small salary and pat my head and say, 'Good boy, he fought for his country'?"

Breakfast stretched into lunch. Others came to the table, some stayed, some only stopped to shake his hand and wish him luck. Most were white men. Ali was holding court, and his mood lightened. Soon his eyes softened and his voice deepened and dropped, signals that he was preparing to play back a vision.

"Ah-leee will return," he intoned. "My ghost will haunt all arenas. The people will watch the fights and they will whisper, 'Hey, Ali could whip that guy. . . . You think so? . . . Sure. . . . No, he couldn't. . . . Wish he'd come out of retirement. . . .' "

He leaned across the table "Twenty-five now, make my comeback at 28. That's not old. Whip 'em all. If I get good food in jail. Don't you think?"

A newcomer to the table said it was all so very sad that such a handsome and gifted young man should have even to contemplate death and imprisonment. Ali straightened, his eyes bright again, perhaps like martyrs' eyes reflecting the licking flames.

"Allah," he said, "okays the adversary to try us. That's how he sees if you're a true believer."

On April 28 [1967], in Houston, Muhammad Ali stood his ground as he had promised. The reaction was unusually swift. Within hours, various boxing commissions summarily cashiered him as world heavyweight champion. Ten days later he was indicted by a Federal grand jury on a charge of refusing to submit to the draft, a felony punishable by 5 years in prison and a $10,000 fine. Three days after his indictment, to which he pleaded "not guilty," a trial was set. . . .

He had become an official enemy of the people.

On Feb. 17, 1966, while he was lounging on the lawn of his rented Miami home, a reporter called to tell him that his draft board had reclassified him 1A and that he would probably be called within weeks. He was shocked. He ranted: "How can they do this without another test to see if I'm any wiser or worser than last time? Why are they gunning for me?"

Bright red television trucks pulled up to the house, confirming the disaster. His fight with Terrell, scheduled for the next month, would have to be canceled, he was told. This reporter, a coincidental visitor that day, watched Ali build up to a loss of full control, as he had done in pre-fight publicity scenes.

"I've got a question," he screamed. "For two years the Government caused me international embarrassment, letting people think I was a nut—sure, it bothered me, and my mother and father suffered—and now they jump up and make me 1A without even an official notification or a test. Why did they let me be considered a nut, an illiterate, for two years?"

He eventually subsided, and questioners pressed, asking Ali about Vietnam. He admitted that he wasn't sure where Vietnam was. They asked him about the Vietcong. He shrugged.

"I got no quarrel with them Vietcong."

It would have been difficult to pick a less appropriate day to say that. On television that afternoon Senator Wayne Morse was accusing Gen. Maxwell D. Taylor, as a representative of the Administration, of having misguided the American public about his "limited" war. Morse predicted that before too long the American people would "repudiate our war in Southeast Asia," and General Taylor replied that Hanoi would be very happy about any dissent in the United States.

The report of Ali's imminent draft, the catalytic agent, turned out to be grossly exaggerated. But brushfire "patriotism" canceled the Terrell bout and drove the champion out of his own country seeking matches. That year, spent fighting in Canada, Britain and Germany, brought him in contact with many people, white and black, who said they shared his anti-war stand and admired his courage. It is doubtful if he actually had an anti-Vietnam war stand other than the Muslim prohibition against serving in "white, Christian wars" of any kind. Elijah himself had been imprisoned as a draft evader during Worgd War II.

Outside the United States, where journalists questioned him with more compassion and crowds offered him more affection, Ali became looser and had time to develop a broader philosophy.

In America, when facing hostility, he might be moved to snap back, in an extremely rare burst of mild profanity: "I get booed and this makes me strong. If everybody said, 'Oh, champ, you is wonderful,' I'd just lay back. But if a guy says, 'Son of a bitch, I hope you get your ass whipped,' I got to beat him and everybody else."

But in London he could softly explain to African and Indian students that those who were against him "don't like me because I'm free. The Negro has always sold himself out for money or women, but I give up everything for what I believe. I'm a free man; I don't belong to anybody."

In America, when a newspaper reported that he had gone downtown to a mosque and "hated behind closed doors," he would snap: "Wish everyone would go and do their hating behind closed doors instead of out on the streets."

But in Europe he took a world view. "Elijah is not teaching hate when he tells us about all the evil things the white man has done, any more than you're teaching hate when you tell about what Hitler did to the Jews. That's not hate, that's history."

A leader among England's colored immigrants, Michael De Freitas, sought him out in London, as did other intellectuals and activists. By the time he returned to fight in America, late in 1966, Muhammad Ali was a symbol of many causes. He was invited to speak on campuses and, recently, at an open-housing rally in Louisville and an antiwar demonstration in Chicago, where he said: "In the ring we have a referee to stop the fight if one man should become too hurt physically. Boxing is nothing like going to war with machine guns, bazookas, hand grenades and bomber airplanes."

Always the hungry eclectic, he was picking up new words like "radical" and "great repercussions" and "the white liberals," although he steadfastly refused to take an overt leadership role other than his preaching duties at Muslim mosques. His draft status provoked public comments by Roy Wilkins (who was unsympathetic), the Rev. Dr. Martin Luther King Jr. and Stokely Carmichael. As the day of his induction approached, pundits and politicians discussed the sophisticated ramifications of his possible refusal to submit to the draft in terms of racial prejudice, religious discrimination, patriotism, national security and civil disobedience.

Ali himself was musing: "When I'm gone, boxing be nothing again. The fans with the cigars and the hats turned down'll be there, but no more housewives and little men on the street and foreign presidents. It's goin' to be back to the fighter who comes to town, smells a flower, visits a hospital, blows a horn and says he's in shape. Old hat. I was the onliest boxer in history people asked questions like a Senator."

He was very calm the last few days before his induction, as befits a man "being tried by Allah." Except for a local Muslim minister, none of his co-religionists showed up in Houston to give him support. The demonstration that Ali counseled against, but perhaps secretly hoped for, never materialized.

In the weeks to come the pressures on Muhammad Ali will increase as his corner, and the corner of his adversary, become crowded with self-appointed supporters. But whatever happens, Muhammad Ali will stand up to it.

He spent 10 years of his life in sacrifice to a cause, the heavyweight championship, and his faith in himself was justified. No man could beat him, and when his title was taken away the New York Civil Liberties Union protested the action as arbitrary, capricious and unprincipled.

Ali took another cause, that of a minority religion, and sacrificed again, giving up untold millions in revenue and divorcing a beautiful woman who would not abide by the sect's standards. Through it all, and under a constant pressure, he always did what he had to do, and never lost the almost magical purity that could believe, "I ain't losing anything but gaining the world."

Topics for Discussion, Research, and Composition

1. Write a paragraph that explains and illustrates any of the following statements:
   "Building a building is building the lives of the workers and dwellers in the building."
   "The buildings determine civilization as the cells of the honeycomb the function of bees."
   "The son and grandson of preachers, he [Frank Lloyd Wright] became a preacher of blueprints."
2. Isadora Duncan referred to herself as "a proud and sensitive child" who found the public school system "as humiliating as a penitentiary." Have you had or have you witnessed a school experience that in any way parallels Isadora Duncan's negative experience? Briefly describe the circumstances of the situation. What courses of action can be taken by a person in the situation you described?
3. There is some hint here of the type of dancing taught and performed by Isadora Duncan.
   a. Try to imagine a group of dancers moving as instructed by her.
   b. Write a list of adjectives that would describe that dancing.
   c. Extend the meaning of each of these adjectives by creating a simile that further reflects that dance style you envision. Examples: bold—as bold as a neon sign; uninhibited—as uninhibited as a child prancing in a puddle
4. Create a "work of art" from everyday items or photographs of items. Select a theme or category of items. Collect as many samples or illustrations as you can. Arrange, construct, and set these items in patterns until you are pleased with the result. Examine your work

after a few days have passed. Does your work give you a new vision or appreciation of these items?

5. What do the words "masculine" and "feminine" mean to you? For each of these words, create a list of activities or actions that you associate with the word. Why would Zan Hagan object to this activity? Show how she would find fault with your placement of the actions and activities you listed.
6. The title of Heavyweight Champion of the World was once taken away from Muhammad Ali, not because he lost a fight, but because he fought against being inducted into the United States Army at a time when that army was fighting in Vietnam. Take a stand on either issue: Ali's decision to fight induction into the army; the boxing association's decision to strip him of his title.

6

Unfinished Business

It is only a matter of time before we can colonize the moon or some other heavenly body. Imagine the opportunity to start again; the opportunity to create the perfect society. Before work can begin on the creation of a new society, it is important to take stock of the conditions under which people live today. What are the drawbacks to our present life? What are the the features of our present world that cause people to be frustrated or unhappy or endangered?

- Pollution? Which of the items that pollute our air would we want to relinquish in order to have cleaner air?
- Chemicals in our food? What would food that did not have artificial coloring and preservatives be like? What would vegetables and fruits that had not been treated with pesticides be like?
- Crime in the streets? What would it cost to eliminate the poverty that breeds crime? Who would pay the price?
- Provincialism and fear of diversity of thought and behavior? How can the media help to expand people's ideas and opinions?
- Great disparities in living and working conditions between rich and poor? Can we eliminate poverty and squalor? Why would many people continue to oppose a fair-sharing of the nation's or the world's wealth?
- Scarcity of fuel resources? Why are people reluctant to cut back on or give up established patterns of living? Why are we more and more dependent on machinery?

If our cities are now populated by people who live in wretched housing set in traffic-clogged streets, if we breathe polluted air and eat chemically injected foods, if we fear walking in parks or even in the streets at night, if our resources are being depleted and our landscapes blighted, if we suffer from great disparities in the quality of life, who is to blame? What can be done? If you do not like what is happening in your world, what are you going to do about it? In what way can you help to attack these problems that exist?

from **Main Street** *by Sinclair Lewis*

The fact that almost every town in America has its Main Street allows Sinclair Lewis's street to extend way beyond the Midwestern town of Gopher Prairie. Carol Kennicott moves there as a bride and immediately faces a problem: How can she adapt to a new social life and retain her individuality? The rest of Main Street, too, has a problem: How do they deal with a woman who has some original ideas?

* * *

The Jolly Seventeen (the membership of which ranged from fourteen to twenty-six) was the social cornice of Gopher Prairie. It was the country club, the diplomatic set, the St. Cecilia, the Ritz oval room, the Club de Vingt. To belong to it was to be "in." Though its membership partly coincided with that of the Thanatopsis study club, the Jolly Seventeen as a separate entity guffawed at the Thanatopsis, and considered it middle-class and even "highbrow."

Most of the Jolly Seventeen were young married women with their husbands as associate members. Once a week they had a women's afternoon-bridge; once a month the husbands joined them for supper and evening-bridge; twice a year they had dances at I.O.O.F. Hall. Then the town exploded. Only at the annual balls of the Firemen and of the Eastern Star was there such prodigality of chiffon scarfs and tangoing and heart-burnings, and these rival institutions were not select—hired girls attended the Firemen's Ball, with section-hands and laborers. Ella Stowbody had once gone to a Jolly Seventeen Soirée in the village hack, hitherto confined to chief mourners at funerals; and Harry Haydock and Dr. Terry Gould always appeared in the town's only specimens of evening clothes.

The afternoon-bridge of the Jolly Seventeen which followed Carol's lonely doubting was held at Juanita Haydock's new concrete bungalow, with its door of polished oak and beveled plate-glass, jar of ferns in the plastered hall, and in the living-room, a fumed oak Morris chair, sixteen color-prints, and a square varnished table with a mat made of cigar-ribbons on which was one Illustrated Gift Edition and one pack of cards in a burnt-leather case.

Carol stepped into a sirocco of furnace heat. They were already playing. Despite her flabby resolves she had not yet learned bridge. She was winningly apologetic about it to Juanita, and ashamed that she should have to go on being apologetic.

Mrs. Dave Dyer, a sallow woman with a thin prettiness, devoted to experiments in religious cults, illnesses, and scandal-bearing, shook her finger at Carol and trilled, "You're a naughty one! I don't believe you appreciate the honor, when you got into the Jolly Seventeen so easy!"

Mrs. Chet Dashaway nudged her neighbor at the second table. But Carol kept up the appealing bridal manner so far as possible. She twittered, "You're perfectly right. I'm a lazy thing. I'll make Will start teaching me this very evening." Her supplication had all the sound of birdies in the nest, and Easter church-bells, and frosted Christmas cards. Internally she snarled, "That ought to be saccharine enough." She sat in the smallest rocking-chair, a model of Victorian modesty. But she saw or she imagined that the women who had gurgled at her so welcomingly when she had first come to Gopher Prairie were nodding at her brusquely.

During the pause after the first game she petitioned Mrs. Jackson Elder, "Don't you think we ought to get up another bob-sled party soon?"

"It's so cold when you get dumped in the snow," said Mrs. Elder, indifferently.

"I hate snow down my neck," volunteered Mrs. Dave Dyer, with an unpleasant look at Carol and, turning her back, she bubbled at Rita Simons, "Dearie, won't you run in this evening? I've got the loveliest new Butterick pattern I want to show you."

Carol crept back to her chair. In the fervor of discussing the game they ignored her. She was not used to being a wallflower. She struggled to keep from oversensitiveness, from becoming unpopular by the sure method of believing that she was unpopular; but she hadn't much reserve of patience, and at the end of the second game, when Ella Stowbody sniffily asked her, "Are you going to send to Minneapolis for your dress for the next soirée—heard you were," Carol said "Don't know yet" with unnecessary sharpness.

She was relieved by the admiration with which the *jeune fille* Rita Simons looked at the steel buckles on her pumps; but she resented Mrs. Howland's tart demand, "Don't you find that new couch of yours is too broad to be practical?" She nodded, then shook her head, and touchily left Mrs. Howland to get out of it any meaning she desired. Immediately she wanted to make peace. She was close to simpering in the sweetness with which she addressed Mrs. Howland: "I think that is the prettiest display of beef-tea your husband has in his store."

"Oh yes, Gopher Prairie isn't so much behind the times," gibed Mrs. Howland. Some one giggled.

Their rebuffs made her haughty; her haughtiness irritated them to franker rebuffs; they were working up to a state of painfully righteous war when they were saved by the coming of food.

Though Juanita Haydock was highly advanced in the matters of finger-bowls, doilies, and bath-mats, her "refreshments" were typical of all the afternoon-coffees. Juanita's best friends, Mrs. Dyer and Mrs. Dashaway, passed large dinner plates, each with a spoon, a fork, and a coffee cup without saucer. They apologized and discussed the afternoon's game as they passed through the thicket of women's feet. Then they distributed hot buttered rolls, coffee poured from an enamel-ware pot, stuffed olives, potato salad, and angel's-food cake. There was, even in the most strictly conforming Gopher Prairie circles, a certain option as to collations. The olives need not be stuffed. Doughnuts were in some houses well thought of as a substitute for the hot buttered rolls. But there was in all the town no heretic save Carol who omitted angel's-food.

They ate enormously. Carol had a suspicion that the thriftier housewives made the afternoon treat do for evening supper.

She tried to get back into the current. She edged over to Mrs. McGanum. Chunky, amiable, young Mrs. McGanum, with her breast and arms of a milkmaid, and her loud delayed laugh which burst startlingly from a sober face, was the daughter of old Dr. Westlake, and the wife of Westlake's partner, Dr. McGanum. Kennicott asserted that Westlake and McGanum and their contaminated families were tricky, but Carol had found them gracious. She asked for friendliness by crying to Mrs. McGanum, "How is the baby's throat now?" and she was attentive while Mrs. McGanum rocked and knitted and placidly described symptoms.

Vida Sherwin came in after school, with Miss Ethel Villets, the town librarian. Miss Sherwin's optimistic presence gave Carol more confidence. She talked. She informed the circle, "I drove almost down to Wahkeenyan with Will, a few days ago. Isn't the country lovely! And I do admire the Scandinavian farmers down there so: their big red barns and silos and milking-machines and everything. Do you all know that lonely Lutheran church, with the tin-covered spire, that stands out alone on a hill? It's so bleak; somehow it seems so brave. I do think the Scandinavians are the hardiest and best people——"

"Oh, do you *think* so?" protested Mrs. Jackson Elder. "My husband says the Svenskas that work in the planing-mill are perfectly terrible—so silent and cranky, and so selfish, the way they keep demanding raises. If they had their way they'd simply ruin the business."

"Yes, and they're simply *ghastly* hired girls!" wailed Mrs. Dave Dyer. "I swear, I work myself to skin and bone trying to please my hired girls—when I can get them! I do everything in the world for them. They can have their gentleman friends call on them in the kitchen any time, and they get just the same to eat as we do, if there's any left over, and I practically never jump on them."

Juanita Haydock rattled, "They're ungrateful, all that class of people. I do think the domestic problem is simply becoming awful. I don't know what the country's coming to, with these Scandahoofian clodhoppers demanding every cent you can save, and so ignorant and impertinent, and on my word, demanding bath-tubs and everything—as if they weren't mighty good and lucky at home if they got a bath in the wash-tub."

They were off, riding hard. Carol thought of Bea and waylaid them:

"But isn't it possibly the fault of the mistresses if the maids are ungrateful? For generations we've given them the leavings of food, and holes to live in. I don't want to boast, but I must say I don't have much trouble with Bea. She's so friendly. The Scandinavians are sturdy and honest——"

Mrs. Dave Dyer snapped, "Honest? Do you call it honest to hold us up for every cent of pay they can get? I can't say that I've had any of them steal anything (though you might call it stealing to eat so much that a roast of beef hardly lasts three days), but just the same I don't intend to let them think they can put anything over on *me!* I always make them pack and unpack their trunks down-stairs, right under my eyes, and then I know they aren't being tempted to dishonesty by any slackness on *my* part!"

"How much do the maids get here?" Carol ventured.

Mrs. B. J. Gougerling, wife of the banker, stated in a shocked manner, "Any place from three-fifty to five-fifty a week! I know positively that Mrs. Clark, after swearing that she wouldn't weaken and encourage them in their outrageous demands, went and paid five-fifty—think of it! practically a dollar a day for unskilled work and, of course, her food and room and a chance to do her own washing right in with the rest of the wash. *How much do you pay, Mrs. Kennicott?*"

"Yes! How much do you pay?" insisted half a dozen.

"W-why, I pay six a week," she feebly confessed.

They gasped. Juanita protested, "Don't you think it's hard on the rest of us when you pay so much?" Juanita's demand was re-inforced by the universal glower.

Carol was angry. "I don't care! A maid has one of the hardest jobs on earth. She works from ten to eighteen hours a day. She has to wash slimy dishes and dirty clothes. She tends the children and runs to the door with wet chapped hands and——"

Mrs. Dave Dyer broke into Carol's peroration with a furious, "That's all very well, but believe me, I do those things myself when I'm without a maid—and that's a good share of the time for a person that isn't willing to yield and pay exorbitant wages!"

Carol was retorting, "But a maid does it for strangers, and all she gets out of it is the pay——"

Their eyes were hostile. Four of them were talking at once. Vida Sherwin's dictatorial voice cut through, took control of the revolution:

"Tut, tut, tut, tut! What angry passions—and what an idiotic discussion! All of you getting too serious. Stop it! Carol Kennicott, you're probably right, but you're too much ahead of the times. Juanita, quit looking so belligerent. What is this, a card party or a hen fight? Carol, you stop admiring yourself as the Joan of Arc of the hired girls, or I'll spank you. You come over here and talk libraries with Ethel Villets. Boooooo! If there's any more pecking, I'll take charge of the hen roost myself!"

They all laughed artificially, and Carol obediently "talked libraries."

A small-town bungalow, the wives of a village doctor and a village dry-goods merchant, a provincial teacher, a colloquial brawl over paying a servant a dollar more a week. Yet this insignificance echoed cellar-plots and cabinet meetings and labor conferences in Persia and Prussia, Rome and Boston, and the orators who deemed themsleves international leaders were but the raised voice of a billion Juanitas denouncing a million Carols, with a hundred thousand Vida Sherwins trying to shoo away the storm.

* * *

"They're too much for me," Carol sighed to Kennicott. "I've been thinking about getting up an annual Community Day, when the whole town would forget feuds and go out and have sports and a picnic and a dance. But Bert Tybee (why did you ever elect him mayor?)—he's kidnapped my idea. He wants the Community Day, but he wants to have some politician 'give an address.' That's just the stilted sort of thing I've tried to avoid. He asked Vida, and of course she agreed with him."

Kennicott considered the matter while he wound the clock and they tramped up-stairs.

"Yes, it would jar you to have Bert butting in," he said amiably. "Are you going to do much fussing over this Community stunt? Don't you ever get tired of fretting and stewing and experimenting?"

"I haven't even started. Look!" She led him to the nursery door, pointed at the fuzzy brown head of her daughter. "Do you see that object on the pillow? Do you know what it is? It's a bomb to blow up smugness. If you Tories were wise, you wouldn't arrest anarchists; you'd arrest all these children while they're asleep in their cribs. Think what that baby will see and meddle with before she dies in the year 2000! She may see an industrial union of the whole world, she may see aeroplanes going to Mars."

"Yump, probably be changes all right," yawned Kennicott.

She sat on the edge of his bed while he hunted through his bureau for a collar which ought to be there and persistently wasn't.

"I'll go on, always. And I am happy. But this Community Day makes me see how thoroughly I'm beaten."

"That darn collar certainly is gone for keeps," muttered Kennicott and, louder, "Yes, I guess you——I didn't quite catch what you said, dear."

She patted his pillows, turned down his sheets, as she reflected:

"But I have won in this: I've never excused my failures by sneering at my aspirations, by pretending to have gone beyond them. I do not admit that Main Street is as beautiful as it should be! I do not admit that Gopher Prairie is greater or more generous than Europe! I do not admit that dish-washing is enough to satisfy all women! I may not have fought the good fight, but I have kept the faith."

"Sure. You bet you have," said Kennicott. "Well, good night. Sort of feels to me like it might snow tomorrow. Have to be thinking about putting up the storm-windows pretty soon. Say, did you notice whether the girl put that screwdriver back?"

"Come!" *by David Ignatow*

This poem immediately exclaims, "The city is insane." Examine all of the elements held up for criticism. If you use this poem as a springboard, you will find that it can be extended into a probe of society in general.

* * *

Come, let us blow up the whole business;
the city is insane.
Let us plant trees, grass and flowers
in the rubble to disguise it.
Let us restore the city to its first aim
of being natural to the touch.

Break down the sordid hospital;
the cockroach-ridden restaurants,
the whore-packed hotels
and business buildings close by for convenience;
the big night clubs and intimate ones
in the cellars of old homes,
where rats and vermin and dark dampness
used to sport.

The stock exchange and the banks
where we sell each other;
the gaudy apartment houses and the broken-down
ones
to which we have been assigned,
each according to his profit;
the gutters where we run each other down;
the sidewalks where we watch with interest.
The stores of adulterated foods
and ready medicines;
the hospitals with an eye towards business
and the doctor's income;
the homes for the aged
where the aged are forgotten.
All this let us demolish once and for all
with a perfect time bomb;
and of course with the formality of a warning
to those who will wish to stay behind.
But let us wipe out a few hundred million.

"Pollution" *by Tom Lehrer*

Tom Lehrer has achieved some fame for having two rather dissimilar professions: He is a college math professor; he is also a songwriter and entertainer. His is the work of the satirist. He, too, takes what he sees as abuses and stupidities and holds them up to ridicule. His format is a song with funny lyrics. Imagine, singing about pollution!

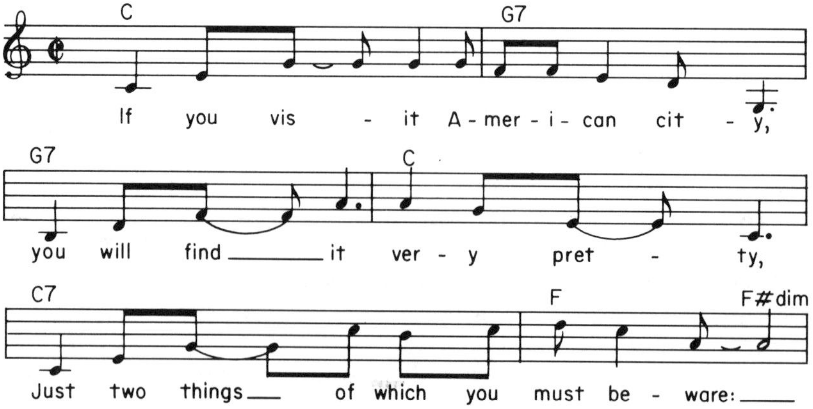

See the halibuts and the sturgeons
Being wiped out by detergeons,
Fish gotta swim and birds gotta fly,
But they don't last long if they try.
POLLUTION, POLLUTION,
You can use the latest toothpaste,
And then rinse your mouth with industrial waste.

Just go out for a breath of air,
And you'll be ready for Medicare,
The city streets are really quite a thrill,
If the hoods don't get you, monoxide will.
POLLUTION, POLLUTION,
Wear a gas mask and a veil,
Then you can breathe long as you don't inhale.

from **The Jungle** *by Upton Sinclair*

These stamps and labels on food indicate that the government has inspected and graded the product. What difference would it make to the producers, processors, and packagers if the government did not monitor their products?

There was a time when the government did not do such inspecting. Upton Sinclair's exposé of the meat industry was instrumental in forcing action. The section printed here did much to arouse the conscience of the public.

* * *

With one member trimming beef in a cannery, and another working in a sausage factory, the family had a first-hand knowledge of the great majority of Packingtown swindles. For it was the custom, as they found, whenever meat was so spoiled that it could not be used for anything else, either to can it or else to chop it up into sausage. With what had been told them by Jonas, who had worked in the pickle-rooms, they could now study the whole of the spoiled-meat industry on the inside, and read a new and grim meaning into that old Packingtown jest—that they use everything of the pig except the squeal.

Jonas had told them how the meat that was taken out of pickle would often be found sour, and how they would rub it up with soda to take away the smell, and sell it to be eaten on free-lunch counters; also of all the miracles of chemistry which they performed, giving to any sort of meat, fresh or salted, whole or chopped, any color and any flavor and any odor they chose. In the pickling of hams they had an ingenious apparatus, by which they saved time and increased the capacity of the plant—a machine consisting of a hollow needle attached to a pump; by plunging this needle into the meat and working with his foot, a man could fill a ham with pickle in a few seconds. And yet, in spite of this, there would be hams found spoiled, some of them with an odor so bad that a man could hardly bear to be in the room with them. To pump into these the packers had a second and much stronger pickle which destroyed the odor—a process known to the workers as "giving them thirty per cent." Also, after the hams had been smoked, there would be found some that had gone to the bad. Formerly these had been sold as "Number Three Grade," but later on some ingenious person had hit upon a new device, and now they would extract the bone, about which the bad part generally lay, and insert in the hole a white-hot iron. After this invention there was no longer Number One, Two, and Three Grade—there was only Number One Grade. The packers were always originating such schemes—they had what they called "boneless hams," which were all the odds and ends of pork stuffed into casings; and "California hams," which were the shoulders, with big knuckle-joints, and nearly all the meat cut out; and fancy "skinned hams," which were made of the oldest hogs, whose skins were so heavy and coarse that no one would buy them—that is, until they had been cooked and chopped fine and labelled "head cheese"!

It was only when the whole ham was spoiled that it came into the department of Elzbieta. Cut up by the two-thousand-revolutions-a-minute flyers, and mixed with half a ton of other meat, no odor that ever was in a ham could make any difference. There was never the least attention paid to what was cut up for sausage; there would come all the way back from Europe old sausage that had been rejected, and that was mouldy and white—it would be dosed with borax and glycerine, and dumped into the hoppers, and made over again for home consumption. There would be meat that had tumbled out on the floor, in the dirt and sawdust, where the workers had tramped and spit uncounted billions of consumption germs. There would be meat stored in great piles in rooms; and the water from leaky roofs would drip over it, and thousands of rats would race about on it. It was too dark in these storage places to see well, but a man could run his hand over these piles of meat and sweep off handfuls of the dried dung of rats. These rats were nuisances, and the packers would put poisoned bread out for them; they would die, and then rats, bread and meat would go into the hoppers together. This is no fairy story and no joke; the meat would be shovelled into carts, and the man who did the shovelling would not trouble to lift out a rat even when he saw one—there were things that went into the sausage in comparison with which a poisoned rat was a tidbit. There was no place for the men to wash their hands before they ate their dinner, and so they made a practice of washing them in the water that was to be ladled into the sausage. There were the butt-ends of smoked meat, and the scraps of corned beef, and all the odds and ends of the waste of the plants, that would be dumped into old barrels in the cellar and left there. Under the system of rigid economy which the packers enforced, there were some jobs that it only paid to do once in a long time, and among these was the cleaning out of the waste-barrels. Every spring they did it; and in the barrels would be dirt and rust and old nails and stale water—and cart load after cart load of it would be taken up and dumped into the hoppers with fresh meat, and sent out to the public's breakfast. Some of it they would make into "smoked" sausage—but as the smoking took time, and was therefore expensive, they would call upon their chemistry department, and preserve it with borax and color it with gelatine to make it brown. All of their sausage came out of the same bowl, but when they came to wrap it they would stamp some of it "special," and for this they would charge two cents more a pound.

from **"Poor Man's Pudding"** *by Herman Melville*

It's hard work to be poor . . . and to survive. What special pressures do the poor feel? How are these seen and interpreted by those who are relatively rich? How do you think poverty affects one's sense of law and order?

* * *

"You see," said poet Blandmour, enthusiastically—as some forty years ago we walked along the road in a soft, moist snow-fall, toward the end of March—"you see, my friend, that the blessed almoner, Nature, is in all things beneficent; and not only so, but considerate in her charities, as any discreet human philanthropist might be. This snow, now, which seems so unseasonable, is in fact just what a poor husbandman needs. Rightly is this soft March snow, falling just before seed-time, rightly is it called 'Poor Man's Manure.' Distilling from kind heaven upon the soil, by a gentle penetration it nourishes every clod, ridge, and furrow. To the poor farmer it is as good as the rich farmer's farm-yard enrichments. And the poor man has no trouble to spread it, while the rich man has to spread his."

"Perhaps so," said I, without equal enthusiasm, brushing some of the damp flakes from my chest. "It may be as you say, dear Blandmour. But tell me, how is it that the wind drives yonder drifts of 'Poor Man's Manure' off poor Coulter's two-acre patch here, and piles it up yonder on rich Squire Teamster's twenty-acre field?"

"Ah! to be sure—yes—well; Coulter's field, I suppose, is sufficiently moist without further moistenings. Enough is as good as a feast, you know."

"Yes," replied I, "of this sort of damp fare," shaking another shower of the damp flakes from my person. "But tell me, this warm spring-snow may answer very well, as you say; but how is it with the cold snows of the long, long winters here?"

"Why, do you not remember the words of the Psalmist?—'The Lord giveth snow like wool;' meaning not only that snow is white as wool, but warm, too, as wool. For the only reason, as I take it, that wool is comfortable, is because air is entangled, and therefore warmed among its fibres. Just so, then, take the temperature of a December field when covered with this snow-fleece, and you will no doubt find it several degrees above that of the air. So, you see, the winter's snow *itself* is beneficent; under the pretense of frost—a sort of gruff philanthropist—actually warming the earth, which afterward is to be fertilizingly moistened by these gentle flakes of March."

"I like to hear you talk, dear Blandmour; and, guided by your benevolent heart, can only wish to poor Coulter plenty of this 'Poor Man's Manure.' "

"But that is not all," said Blandmour, eagerly. "Did you never hear of the 'Poor Man's Eye-water?' "

"Never."

Take this soft March snow, melt it, and bottle it. It keeps pure as alcohol. The very best thing in the world for weak eyes. I have a whole demijohn for it myself. But the poorest man, afflicted in his eyes, can freely help himself to this same all-bountiful remedy. Now, what a kind provision is that!"

"Then 'Poor Man's Manure' is 'Poor Man's Eye-water' too?"

"Exactly. And what could be more economically contrived? One thing answering two ends—ends so very distinct."

"Very distinct, indeed."

"Ah! that is your way. Making sport of earnest. But never mind. We have been talking of snow; but common rain-water—such as falls all the year round—is still more kindly. Not to speak of its known fertilizing quality as to fields, consider it in one of its minor lights. Pray, did you ever hear of a 'Poor Man's Egg?' "

"Never. What is that, now?"

"Why, in making some culinary preparations of meal and flour, where eggs are recommended in the receipt-book, a substitute for the eggs may be had in a cup of cold rain-water, which acts as leaven. And so a cup of cold rain-water thus used is called by housewives a 'Poor Man's Egg.' And many rich men's housekeepers sometimes use it."

"But only when they are out of hen's eggs, I presume, dear Blandmour. But your talk is—I sincerely say it—most agreeable to me. Talk on."

"Then there's 'Poor Man's Plaster' for wounds and other bodily harms; an alleviative and curative, compounded of simple, natural things; and so, being so very cheap, is accessible to the poorest of sufferers. Rich men often use 'Poor Man's Plaster.' "

"But not without the judicious advice of a fee'd physician, dear Blandmour."

"Doubtless, they first consult the physician; but that may be an unnecessary precaution."

"Perhaps so. I do not gainsay it. Go on."

"Well, then, did you ever eat of a 'Poor Man's Pudding?' "

"I never so much as heard of it before."

"Indeed! Well, now you shall eat of one; and you shall eat it, too, as made, unprompted, by a poor man's wife, and you shall eat it at a poor man's table, and in a poor man's house. Come now, and if after this ating, you do not say that a 'Poor Man's Pudding' is as relishable as a rich man's, I will give up the point altogether; which briefly is: that, through kind Nature, the poor, out of their very poverty, extract comfort."

Not to narrate any more of our conversations upon this subject (for we had several—I being at that time the guest of Blandmour in the country, for the benefit of my health), suffice it that, acting upon Blandmour's hint, I introduced myself into Coulter's house on a wet Monday noon (for the snow had thawed), under the innocent pretense of craving a pedestrian's rest and refreshment for an hour or two.

I was greeted, not without much embarrassment—owing, I suppose, to my dress—but still with unaffected and honest kindness. Dame Coulter was just leaving the wash-tub to get ready her one o'clock meal against her good man's return from a deep wood about a mile distant among the hills, where he was chopping by day's-work—seventy-five cents per day—and found himself. The washing being done outside the main building, under an infirm-looking old shed, the dame stood upon a half-rotten, soaked board to protect her feet, as well as might be, from the penetrating damp of the bare ground; hence she looked pale and chill. But her paleness had still another and more secret cause—the paleness of a mother to be. A quiet fathomless heart-trouble, too, couched beneath the mild, resigned blue of her soft and wife-like eye. But she smiled upon me, as apologizing for the unavoidable disorder of a Monday and a washing-day, and, conducting me into the kitchen, set me down in the best seat it had—an old-fashioned chair of an enfeebled constitution.

I thanked her; and sat rubbing my hands before the ineffectual low fire, and—unobservantly as I could—glancing now and then about the room, while the good woman, throwing on more sticks, said she was sorry the room was no warmer. Something more she said, too—not repiningly, however—of the fuel, as old and damp; picked-up sticks in Squire Teamster's forest, where her husband was chopping the sappy logs of the living tree for the Squire's fires. It needed not her remark, whatever it was, to convince me of the inferior quality of the sticks; some being quite mossy and toad-stooled with long lying bedded among the accumulated dead leaves of many autumns. They made a sad hissing, and vain spluttering enough.

"You must rest yourself here till dinner-time, at least," said the dame; "what I have you are heartily welcome to."

I thanked her again, and begged her not to heed my presence in the least, but go on with her usual affairs.

I was struck by the aspect of the room. The house was old, and constitutionally damp. The window-sills had beads of exuded dampness upon them. The shriveled sashes shook in their frames, and the green panes of glass were clouded with the long thaw. On some little errand the dame passed into an adjoining chamber, leaving the door partly open. The floor of that room was carpetless, as the kitchen's was. Nothing but bare necessaries were about me; and those not of the best sort. Not a print on the wall; but an old volume of Doddridge lay on the smoked chimney-shelf.

"You must have walked a long way, sir; you sigh so with weariness."

"No, I am not nigh so weary as yourself, I dare say."

"Oh, but I am accustomed to that; *you* are not, I should think," and her soft, sad blue eye ran over my dress. "But I must sweep these shavings away; husband made him a new axe-helve this morning before sunrise, and I have been so busy washing, that I have had no time to clear up. But now they are just the thing I want for the fire. They'd be much better though, were they not so green."

Now if Blandmour were here, thought I to myself, he would call those green shavings "Poor Man's Matches," or "Poor Man's Tinder," or some pleasant name of that sort.

"I do not know," said the good woman, turning round to me again—as she stirred among her pots on the smoky fire—"I do not know how you will like our pudding. It is only rice, milk, and salt boiled together."

"Ah, what they call 'Poor Man's Pudding,' I suppose you mean."

A quick flush, half resentful, passed over her face.

"*We* do not call it so, sir," she said, and was silent.

Upbraiding myself for my inadvertence, I could not but again think to myself what Blandmour would have said, had he heard those words and seen that flush.

At last a slow, heavy footfall was heard; then a scraping at the door, and another voice said, "Come, wife; come, come—I must be back again in a jiff—if you say I *must* take all my meals at home, you must be speedy; because the Squire—Good day, sir," he exclaimed, now first catching sight of me as he entered the room. He turned toward his wife, inquiringly, and stood stock-still, while the moisture oozed from his patched boots to the floor.

"This gentleman stops here awhile to rest and refresh: he will take dinner with us, too. All will be ready now in a trice; so sit down on the bench, husband, and be patient, I pray. You see sir," she continued, turning to me, "William there wants, of mornings, to carry a cold meal into the woods with him, to save the long one o'clock walk across the fields to and fro. But I won't let him. A warm dinner is more than pay for the long walk."

"I don't know about that," said William, shaking his head. "I have often debated in my mind whether it really paid. There's not much odds, either way, between a wet walk after hard work, and a wet dinner before it. But I like to oblige a good wife like Martha. And you know, sir, that women will have their whimsies."

"I wish they all had as kind whimsies as your wife has," said I.

"Well, I've heard that some women ain't all maple-sugar; but, content with dear Martha, I don't know much about others."

"You find rare wisdom in the woods," mused I.

"Now, husband, if you ain't too tired, just lend a hand to draw the table out."

"Nay," said I, "let him rest, and let me help."

"No," said William, rising.

"Sit still," said his wife to me.

The table set, in due time we all found ourselves with plates before us.

"You see what we have," said Coulter—"salt pork, rye-bread, and pudding. Let me help you. I got this pork of the Squire; some of his last year's pork, which he let me have on account. It isn't quite so sweet as this year's would be; but I find it hearty enough to work on, and that's all I eat for. Only let the rheumatiz and other sicknesses keep clear of me, and I ask no flavors of favors from any. But you don't eat of the pork!"

"I see," said the wife, gently and gravely, "that the gentleman knows the difference between this year's and last year's pork. But perhaps he will like the pudding."

I summoned up all my self-control, and smilingly assented to the proposition of the pudding, without by my looks casting any reflections upon the pork. But, to tell the truth, it was quite impossible for me (not being ravenous, but only a little hungry at the time) to eat of the latter, It had a yellowish crust all round it, and was rather rankish, I thought, to the taste. I observed, too, that the dame did not eat of it, though she suffered some to be put on her plate, and pretended to be busy with it when Coulter looked that way. But she ate of the rye-bread, and so did I.

"Now, then, for the pudding," said Coulter. "Quick, wife; the Squire sits in his sitting-room window, looking far out across the fields. His time-piece is true."

"He don't play the spy on you, does he?" said I.

"Oh, no!—I don't say that. He's a good enough man. He gives me work. But he's particular. Wife, help the gentleman. You see, sir, if I lose the Squire's work, what will become of—" and, with a look for which I honored humanity, with sly significance he glanced toward his wife; then, a little changing his voice, instantly continued—"that fine horse I am going to buy."

"I guess," said the dame, with a strange, subdued sort of inefficient pleasantry—"I guess that fine horse you sometimes so merrily dream of will long stay in the Squire's stall. But sometimes his man gives me a Sunday ride."

"A Sunday ride!" said I.

"You see," resumed Coulter, "wife loves to go to church; but the nighest is four miles off, over yon snowy hills. So she can't walk it; and I can't carry her in my arms, though I have carried her up-stairs before now. But, as she says, the Squire's man sometimes gives her a lift on the road; and for this cause it is that I speak of a horse I am going to have one of these fine sunny days. And already, before having it, I have christened it 'Martha.' But what am I about? Come, come, wife! the pudding! Help the gentleman, do! The Squire! the Squire!—think of the Squire! and help round the pudding. There, one—two—three mouthfuls must do me. Good-bye, wife. Good-bye, sir. I'm off."

And, snatching his soaked hat, the noble Poor Man hurriedly went out into the soak and the mire.

I suppose now, thinks I to myself, that Blandmour would poetically say, He goes to take a Poor Man's Saunter.

"You have a fine husband," said I to the woman, as we were now left together.

"William loves me this day as on the wedding-day, sir. Some hasty words, but never a harsh one. I wish I were better and stronger for his sake. And, oh! sir, both for his sake and mine," (and the soft, blue, beautiful eyes turned into two well-springs) "how I wish little William and Martha lived—it is so lonely-like now. William named after him, and Martha for me."

When a companion's heart of itself overflows, the best one can do is to do nothing. I sat looking down on my as yet untasted pudding.

"You should have seen little William, sir. Such a bright, manly boy, only six years old—cold, cold now!"

Plunging my spoon into the pudding, I forced some into my mouth to stop it.

"And little Martha—Oh! sir, she was the beauty! Bitter, bitter! but needs must be borne."

The mouthful of pudding now touched my palate, and touched it with a mouldy, briny taste. The rice, I knew, was of that damaged sort sold cheap; and the salt from the last year's pork barrel.

"Ah, sir, if those little ones yet to enter the world were the same little ones which so sadly have left it; returning friends, not strangers, strangers, always strangers! Yet does a mother soon learn to love them; for certain, sir, they come from where the others have gone. Don't you believe that, sir? Yes, I know all good people must. But, still, still—and I fear it is wicked, and very black-hearted, too—still, strive how I may to cheer me with thinking of little William and Martha in heaven, and with reading Dr. Doddridge there—still, still does dark grief leak in, just like the rain through our roof. I am left so lonesome now; day after day, all the day long, dear William is gone; and all the damp day long grief drizzles and drizzles down on my soul. But I pray to God to forgive me for this; and for the rest, manage it as well as I may."

Bitter and mouldy is the "Poor Man's Pudding," groaned I to myself, half choked with but one little mouthful of it, which would hardly go down.

I could stay no longer to hear of sorrows for which the sincerest sympathies could give no adequate relief; of a fond persuasion, to which there could be furnished no further proof than already was had—a persuasion, too, of that sort which much speaking is sure more or less to mar; of causeless self-upbraidings, which no expostulations could have dispelled. I offered no pay for hospitalities gratuitous and honorable as those of a prince. I knew that such offerings would have been more than declined; charity resented.

The native American poor never lose their delicacy or pride; hence, though unreduced to the physical degradation of the European pauper, they yet suffer more in mind than the poor of any other people in the world. Those peculiar social sensibilities nourished by our own peculiar political principles, while they enhance the true dignity of a prosperous American, do but minister to the added wretchedness of the unfortunate; first, by prohibiting their acceptance of what little random relief charity may offer; and, second, by furnishing them with the keenest appreciation of the smarting distinction between their ideal of universal equality and their grindstone experience of the practical misery and infamy of poverty—a misery and infamy which is, ever has been, and ever will be, precisely the same in India, England, and America.

Under pretense that my journey called me forthwith, I bade the dame good-bye; shook her cold hand; looked my last into her blue, resigned eye, and went out into the wet. But cheerless as it was, and damp, damp, damp—the heavy atmosphere charged with all sorts of incipiencies—I yet became conscious, by the suddenness of the contrast, that the house air I had quitted was laden down with that peculiar deleterious quality, the height of which—insufferable to some visitants—will be found in a poor-house ward.

This ill-ventilation in winter of the rooms of the poor—a thing, too, so stubbornly persisted in—is usually charged upon them as their disgraceful neglect of the most simple means to health. But the instinct of the poor is wiser than we think. The air which ventilates, likewise *cools*. And to any shiverer, ill-ventilated warmth is better than well-ventilated cold. Of all the preposterous assumptions of humanity over humanity, nothing exceeds most of the criticisms made on the habits of the poor by the well-housed, well-warmed, and well-fed.

* * *

"Blandmour," said I that evening, as after tea I sat on his comfortable sofa, before a blazing fire, with one of his two ruddy little children on my knee, "you are not what may rightly be called a rich man; you have a fair competence; no more. Is it not so? Well, then, I do not include *you,* when I say, that if ever a Rich Man speaks prosperously to me of a Poor Man, I shall set it down as—I won't mention the word."

from **Cesar Chavez, Autobiography of La Causa**
by Jacques E. Levy

Jesus preached and practiced nonviolence. Gandhi preached and practiced nonviolence. Martin Luther King, Jr. preached and practiced nonviolence. Cesar Chavez preaches and practices nonviolence.

An eye for an eye? Turn the other cheek? What does each method accomplish?

* * *

Cesar Chavez Recalls

To us the boycott of grapes was the most near-perfect of nonviolent struggles, because nonviolence also requires mass involvement. The boycott demonstrated to the whole country, the whole world, what people can do by nonviolent action.

Nonviolence in the abstract is a very difficult thing to comprehend or explain. I'd read a lot, but all of it was in the abstract. It's difficult to carry the message to people who aren't involved. Nonviolence must be explained in context.

People equate nonviolence with inaction—with not doing anything—and it's not that at all. It's exactly the opposite.

In his autobiography, Malcolm X said, "I believe it's a crime for anyone who is being brutalized to continue to accept that brutality without doing something to defend himself. If that's how Christian philosophy is interpreted, if that's what Gandhian philosophy teaches, well then I will call them criminal philosophies."

But Gandhi never said not to do anything. He said exactly the opposite. He said, "Do something! Offer your life!" He said, "If you really want to do something, be willing to die for it." That's asking for the maximum contribution.

Often only talk results when a person with social concern wants to do something for the underdog nonviolently. But just talking about change is not going to bring it about. Talk just gives people an out. Generally what happens is that people will study nonviolence, read books, go to seminars where they discuss nonviolence, and attend endless meetings. In most cases, they find some satisfaction in this and think they somehow are accomplishing something. But all the while, and right across town, the pot is brewing.

Reading is not bad, but thinking they made a great accomplishment is bad. They're kidding themselves. These people can't be effective. Nonviolence becomes just an ideology, something to write about, or read about, or talk about while still being very comfortable. The ideology becomes a luxury, not a way of life. And nothing can be changed while being comfortable. Life is not made that way.

Nonviolence is action. Like anything else, though, it's got to be organized. There must be rules. There must be people following.

The whole essence of nonviolent action is getting a lot of people involved, vast numbers doing little things. It's difficult to get people involved in a picket line, because it takes their time. But any time a person can be persuaded not to eat a grape—and we persuaded millions not to eat grapes—that's involvement, that's the most direct action, and it's set up in such a way that everybody can participate.

Nonviolence also has one big demand—the need to be creative, to develop strategy. Gandhi described it as moral jujitsu. Always hit the opposition off balance, but keep your principles.

Strategy for nonviolence takes a tremendous amout of our time—strategy against the opposition, and strategy to strengthen our support. We can't let people get discouraged. If there's no progress, they say nonviolence doesn't work. They begin to go each and everywhere. And it's only when they are desperate that people think violence is necessary.

Of course, it isn't. If any movement is on the move, violence is the last thing that's wanted.

Naturally, nonviolence takes time. But poverty has been with us since the beginning of time. We just have to work for improvement, I despise exploitation and I want change, but I'm willing to pay the price in terms of time. There's a Mexican saying, "Hay más tiempo que vida"—There's more time than life. We've got all the time in the world.

Some great nonviolent successes have been achieved in history. Moses is about the best example, and the first one. Christ also is a beautiful example, as is the way the Christians overcame tyranny. They needed over three hundred years, but they did it. The most recent example is Gandhi. To me that's the most beautiful one. We can examine it more closely because it happened during our lifetime. It's fantastic how he got so many people to do things, which is the whole essence of nonviolent action.

Nonviolence has the power to attract people and to generate power. That's what happened to Gandhi. Besides millions of Indians, he had many Englishmen, both in England and even India siding with him.

By and large, people oppose violence. So when government or growers use violence against us, we strategize around it. We can respond nonviolently, because that swings people to our side, and that gives us our strength.

First, of course, the workers have to understand nonviolence. Gandhi once said he'd rather have a man be violent than be a coward. I agree. If he's a coward, then what good is he for anyone? But it is our job to see he's not a coward. That's really the beginning point of our training.

And while the philosophy of nonviolence covers physical, verbal, and moral behavior, we haven't achieved that goal. If we can achieve it, we're saints—which we're not. We're still working on eliminating physical violence, though that isn't all, by any stretch of the imagination. After workers begin to understand physical nonviolence among people, then we also apply it to property and go on from there.

It's like a leader marching at the head of a column, going up and down hills. Pretty soon there are forks and cross-streets, and the leader can't be followed because they can't see him. They don't know where he went. The important thing is to bring them along. The important thing is not to get lost.

"Statement to the Court" *by Eugene Debs*

Eugene V. Debs ran for President of the United States on the Socialist party ticket five times (in 1900, 1904, 1908, 1912, and 1920). He twice went to jail, both times on matters of conscience. (While in jail he polled almost a million votes for the presidency in 1920.) What could he have wanted to accomplish that took him down two such diverse roads?

* * *

Your honor, years ago I recognized my kinship with all living beings, and I made up my mind that I was not one bit better than the meanest on earth. I said then, and I say now, that while there is a lower class, I am in it, while there is a criminal element, I am of it, and while there is a soul in prison, I am not free.

I listened to all that was said in this court in support and justification of this prosecution, but my mind remains unchanged. I look upon the Espionage Law as a despotic enactment in flagrant conflict with democratic principles and with the spirit of free institutions. . . .

Your Honor, I have stated in this court that I am opposed to the social system in which we live; that I believe in a fundamental change—but if possible by peaceable and orderly means. . . .

Standing here this morning, I recall my boyhood. At fourteen I went to work in a railroad shop; at sixteen I was firing a freight engine on a railroad. I remember all the hardships and privations of that earlier day, and from that time until now my heart has been with the working class. I could have been in Congress long ago. I have preferred to go to prison. . . .

I am thinking this morning of the men in the mills and factories; of the men in the mines and on the railroads. I am thinking of the women who for a paltry wage are compelled to work out their barren lives; of the little children who in this system are robbed of their childhood and in their tender years are seized in the remorseless grasp of Mammon and forced into the industrial dungeons, there to feed the monster machines while they themselves are being starved and stunted, body and soul. I see them dwarfed and diseased and their little lives broken and blasted because in this high noon of our twentieth-century Christian civilization money is still so much more important than the flesh and blood of childhood. In very truth gold is god today and rules with pitiless sway in the affairs of men.

In this country—the most favored beneath the bending skies—we have vast areas of the richest and most fertile soil, material resources in inexhaustible abundance, the most marvelous productive machinery on earth, and millions of eager workers ready to apply their labor to that machinery to produce in abundance for every man, woman, and child—and if there are still vast numbers of our people who are the victims of poverty and whose lives are an unceasing struggle all the way from youth to old age, until at last death comes to their rescue and stills their aching hearts and lulls these hapless victims to dreamless sleep, it is not the fault of the Almighty: it cannot be charged to nature, but it is due entirely to the outgrown social system in which we live, that ought to be abolished not only in the interest of the toiling masses but in the higher interest of all humanity. . . .

I believe, Your Honor, in common with all Socialists, that this nation ought to own and control its own industries. I believe, as all Socialists do, that all things that are jointly needed and used ought to be jointly owned—that industry, the basis of our social life, instead of being the private property of the few and operated for their enrichment, ought to be the common property of all, democratically administered in the interest of all. . . .

I am opposing a social order in which it is possible for one man who does absolutely nothing that is useful to amass a fortune of hundreds of millions of dollars, while millions of men and women who work all the days of their lives secure barely enough for a wretched existence.

This order of things cannot always endure. I have registered my protest against it. I recognize the feebleness of my effort, but fortunately I am not alone. There are multiplied thousands of others who, like myself, have come to realize that before we may truly enjoy the blessings of civilized life, we must reorganize society upon a mutual and co-operative basis; and to this end we have organized a great economic and political movement that spreads over the face of all the earth.

There are today upwards of sixty millions of Socialists, loyal, devoted adherents to this cause, regardless of nationality, race, creed, color, or sex. They are all making common cause. They are spreading with tireless energy the propaganda of the new social order. They are waiting, watching, and working hopefully through all the hours of the day and the night. They are still in a minority. But they have learned how to be patient and to bide their time. They feel—they know, indeed—that the time is coming, in spite of all opposition, all persecution, when this emancipating gospel will spread among all the peoples, and when this minority will become the triumphant majority and, sweeping into power, inaugurate the greatest social and economic change in history.

In that day we shall have the universal commonwealth—the harmonious co-operation of every nation with every other nation on earth. . . .

Your Honor, I ask no mercy and I plead for no immunity. I realize that finally the right must prevail. I never so clearly comprehended as now the great struggle between the powers of greed and exploitation on the one hand and upon the other the rising hosts of industrial freedom and social justice.

I can see the dawn of the better day for humanity. The people are awakening. In due time they will and must come to their own. . . .

I am now prepared to receive your sentence.

What Price Nuclear Energy?

One of the major concerns facing the public in the 1980s is the use of nuclear energy. Do nuclear energy facilities endanger the public? Is nuclear energy the source for the future? There is a clear conflict of opinion here, one that can arouse strong emotions.

This small notice appeared in a New York newspaper during the first week in August in 1979. If you had read it, or one similar to it, how would you have responded?

* * *

On Sunday the protest against nuclear power moves to Westchester where a coalition of 14 New York groups will demonstrate at the Indian Point nuclear power plants, in Buchanan, about 25 miles from New York City.

A rally will begin at 1 p.m. at the Blue Mountain Reservation in Peekskill—with speakers, music, energy exhibits—culminating in a march to the plant site at 3. At 4 p.m., demonstrators will stage a "die-in," dramatizing the fatal effects of radiation, at the entrances to the site while others will enter the site by climbing fences and other means. Supporters nearby will observe the civil disobedience, the first such action at an operating nuclear power plant on the East Coast.

Indian Point units #1 and #2 are owned by Con Edison and have one of the worst safety records in the country. Unit #2 has had 146 unscheduled shutdowns since 1976—one every seven days.

The demonstration takes place during the 34th anniversary of the bombings of Hiroshima and Nagasaki and relates the dangers of nuclear power to nuclear weapons production.

Buses to the Indian Point rally will leave from six locations in New York. Call Mobilization for Survival (673-1808) or the SHAD Alliance (475-4539) for tickets, and on Long Island call the SHAD Alliance at (516) 360-0045.

Susan Jaffe
from the *Village Voice,* August 1979

* * *

Now read the newspaper articles that appeared the day after the demonstration. How did the people who opposed nuclear energy plants make their opposition known and felt? Did they do this in more than one way? How should police respond to protesters? How did the police respond in this instance?

* * *

★★★★ **DAILY NEWS** Sunny and pleasant today. High in mid 80s. Hot tomorrow. Details on page 67.

Vol. 61. No. 36 New York, Monday, August 6, 1979 Price 25 cents

125 ARRESTED AT INDIAN POINT

3,000 nuke foes stage protest

Nab 125 nuke foes at Indian Point

By RICHARD EDMONDS

About 3,000 antinuclear demonstrators marched on the Indian Point power plants in Westchester yesterday. At least 125 were arrested after climbing a 10-foot cyclone fence and lying down on the ground. there was no violence.

Another 100 demonstrators stretched out outside the gate in what they termed a "die-in," simulating death by radiation to commemorate the 34th anniversary today of the Hiroshima bombing.

After a spirited rally in Blue Mountain State Park about a mile and half away, the demonstrators paraded through Buchanan to the plant where many planned to be arrested on trespassing charges. Some attempted to snarl legal procedures by refusing to give their names.

All arrested were taken to Westchester Community College in Valhalla where those refusing to identify themselves were jailed and the others arraigned.

American tradition

One man in his 30s said, "We're all here as a matter of conscience. Civil disobedience is a good old American tradition."

About 600 cops from the state, Westchester County and local communities were poised in the park, along the line of march and at the Indian Point plants to control the crowd.

"Can happen here"

"Everything that happened at Three Mile Island can happen here — but worse — because the built-up radiation levels are much higher at Indian Point," the gathering was told by Connie Hogarth of the Westchester Peoples Action Coalition, one of the rally's sponsors.

Tom Monaster/Daily News

A demonstrator is taken into custody after climbing 10-foot fence at Indian Point.

She urged the crowd to "lick this dead-end technology" and to "break the stranglehold of multinational corporations like Exxon, Getty, General Electric and Westinghouse."

The rally was part of a national protest in more than 70 cities and at nuclear sites across the nation organized by Mobilization for Survival, a national antinuclear group.

Several thousand demonstrators also gathered in Salem County in the southern part of New Jersey to picket three nuclear power plants in Lower Alloways Creek Township.

The targets of that protest were the plants called Salem I, Salem II and the Hope Creek Station on Lower Alloways Creek.

Calls plants "tip of iceberg"

Hogarth called nuclear power plants "only the tip of the iceberg — the concealed part of that iceberg are neutron bombs, the MX missile and the Trident weapons system."

Cheered enthusiastically by youthful protesters wearing "No Nuke" T-shirts, a family from Harrisburg — near Three Mile Island — told the throng that they "literally live in fear" of the Pennsylvania plant.

"When the accident happened, my family was scared," said 10-year-old Missy McCaughn. "We didn't know whether we would ever see our house or family again."

"Metropolitan Edison and the Nuclear Regulatory Commission are playing with your lives," added her mother, Kathy. "Look out folks — it could happen to you."

Her husband Keith, said: "You get up in the morning, grab the newspaper and say, 'What have they done now?'"

The cyclone fence climbed by the demonstrators was erected in anticipation of antinuclear protests at a cost of more than $700,000. The cost was shared by Con Edison and the state, according to a Con Ed spokesman.

Organizers used tactics designed to cost the utilities and the town money, including having demonstrators get arrested in "dribs and drabs" to force police into overtime.

Buchanan Mayor George Begany told reporters the town intends to sue organizers for the estimated $100,000 the rally will cost the community.

The demonstrations commemorated the World War II bombing of the Japanese cities of Hiroshima on Aug. 6 and of Nagasaki on Aug. 9 in 1945. Japan surrendered Aug. 15.

The targets of the demonstrators were the Indian Point Plants No. 2 and 3, both nuclear reactors, in the town of Buchanan on the Hudson River.

A third Indian Point Plant — No. 1 — closed in 1974 because it lacked an emergency core cooling system.

Indian Point No. 2 is operated by Consolidated Edison, and No. 3 is run by the State Power Authority.

A Power Authority spokesman called No. 3 "virtually problem-free" and said it has been producing electric power for the last 117 days.

Topics for Discussion, Research, and Composition

1. Describe the habits, manners, and beliefs of the Jolly Seventeen of *Main Street.* How does Carol Kennicott avoid becoming a full-fledged member of the group? Why do you suppose she attends the meetings at all? Some people make their protest known by refusing to join a group. Others prefer to join to try to change the group from within. Explain the ways in which each approach can be effective.
2. a. Whether or not you live in a city, you may be only too aware of the conditions David Ignatow denounces in "Come!" If you can, give specific examples from newspaper or TV accounts or your own first- or second-hand experiences. What do you make of his solution to the "whole business"? How serious is he? What meanings are there to "serious"? How serious are you?
   b. What effect do you think a poem like Ignatow's or a speech like Debs's has on you or your classmates, in both the short and long terms?
3. "Big Brother is watching you." This slogan, from the novel *1984*, has come to represent governmental involvement—really overinvolvement—in the lives of citizens. In each of the following areas, determine (a) why it has become necessary, or why the government thinks it has become necessary, for such involvement; (b) what would happen if the government were not involved; (c) why some people or groups object to this involvement.
   - packaging and labeling of foods
   - advertising standards
   - gasoline mileage
   - speed limits
   - working conditions in businesses
   - abortion rights
   - membership in some organizations
   - rights in hiring and promotion
   - right to live where one pleases
   - drinking age
   - equal access to funds for athletics in schools and colleges
4. a. It's often important to try to get the support of people who are undecided or uncommitted. What effect do nonviolent confrontations or protests have on such people? How does this explain the success of Gandhi, King, Chavez, and others who have led nonviolent protests?

b. Find out what you can about the extent of pacifist activities in this country in this century. Your school librarian should be able to suggest where to get information. How effective has pacifist activity been in wartime? In peacetime?

5. John Steinbeck's novel, *The Grapes of Wrath,* written in the 1930s, indicted the country for "crimes" committed against migrant workers in the United States. Decades later, conditions remained relatively unchanged. Cesar Chavez has worked to mobilize farm workers in California so they would have the strength and leverage to negotiate with their employers. Use the *Reader's Guide to Periodical Literature* or *The New York Times Index* to locate articles from the 1970s that trace the progress made by Chavez and the United Farm Workers.
6. Find out what has happened to some of the "rebels" of the 1960s. Use the *Reader's Guide to Periodical Literature* and *The New York Times Index* and ask the school or public librarian for help. Are certain people and groups still active? Have their views changed? If so, how and why? Different class members can research different people and groups. Your teacher or librarian can suggest some.

CONCLUSION

William Bradford
Roger Williams
Anne Hutchinson
Sam Adams
Abigail Adams
Thomas Paine
Ralph Waldo Emerson
Sojourner Truth
Elizabeth Cady Stanton
Amelia Bloomer
Lucy Stone
Nat Turner
Harriet Tubman
Henry David Thoreau
John Brown
Eugene Debs
Dorothy Day
Walt Whitman
Dorothea Dix
Lillian Wald
Samuel Gompers
William Jennings Bryan
John Spargo
Charlotte Perkins Gilman
Isadora Duncan
Frank Lloyd Wright
Andy Warhol
John Cage
Cesar Chavez
Dennis Banks
Buffy Sainte-Marie
Chaney, Goodman, and Schwerner
Ralph Nader
Malcolm X
Tom Hayden

All of these people, some of whom appear in this book, have at some time been called rebels. All of them have taken stands on issues and have had to live with the consequences of their actions. Use the resources of your school and library to find out what they said and did to be classified as rebels; find out what happened to them as a result.

Why did they want to get involved? A good answer may be another question: what would have happened to them if they had remained silent or had taken no action? Would the inner torment then be greater than any of the external difficulties they encountered? It is difficult to calculate the enormous success they enjoyed when they were successful or the equally valuable sense of satisfaction they may have felt at being part of a movement and knowing important work was being done.

If the work and issues were so important, why did they encounter personal difficulties in their work? Some of them were ridiculed, some were jailed, some were executed; most of them, however, were eventually rewarded or even ultimately revered. America, it seems, does not always know what to do with its rebels, or sometimes has a peculiar way of treating them.

Why is this so? This country we know was cradled in a revolutionary rebellion and nurtured on the pioneer spirit of individualism. As a result, we root for the underdog and admire anyone with spunk. The rebel, though, is really a threat, almost so by definition, and therefore is kept at arm's length. The rebel threatens people's comfort and challenges their ideals. As a result, the rebel is first regarded with suspicion and even fear.

Why is it possible for the renegade to eventually become highly regarded? We would be likely to imprison, for example, anyone who would now follow Thoreau's example and withhold all or part of owed tax payments. Many would probably still regard with suspicion anyone who leads a singular, solitary life. But we can now admire and even applaud Thoreau's courage and audacity. Why is Thoreau's rebellion now safe? Why is the outcast now a hero? Why do we canonize the rebel in America?

How does this affect your spirit of independence, your ability to speak up for your beliefs? Re-examine the questionnaire you answered in the introduction. See which of the items you responded to negatively you would now be willing to attempt. Again examine today's newspaper to see how issues are related to your life. How are you going to make certain that your voice is heard and that your opinion is regarded?